Recom

Daniel King is a Biblical scholar who addresses his topics with research, passion and most of all with the anointing of the Holy Spirit. *Grace Wins* is much more than an argument from theology. This book contains eternal truths that Daniel has tested, both personally and in his great outreach to people around the world. Like the apostle Paul, he has experienced that grace that causes us to labor more abundantly. The reader is in for a life-transforming encounter with the grace of God.

- **Peter Youngren**, World Impact Ministries

I have learned from experience that there are two sides to every story. Brother Daniel has definitely explained both sides of the message on Grace. Many of my questions on the teaching of Grace were answered and I know many of yours will be answered also as you read this compelling book.

- **Dr. Buddy Bell**, Ministry of Helps International

Grace. It compels yet never imposes. It is priceless, but without limit. It is essential to life nevertheless still mystifies. We are all indebted to grace and sustained by grace, but do we understand grace? In his stirring book, *Grace Wins*, Daniel King does a masterful job of making the subject of grace both relevant and personally relatable. I encourage you to read this book, immerse yourself in the study of grace and become amazed by this marvelous gift.

- **Dr. Dave Martin**, America's #1 Christian Success Coach and author of The Force of Favor.

On multiple occasions I have been privileged to minister alongside Daniel in nations around the world, and he has taught me how to walk in the grace of God. Grace Wins will give believers and nonbelievers alike a true understanding of the message of grace. In the midst of a church culture that debates this topic so frequently, Daniel does a masterful job of correctly dividing the Word of Truth and looking to the Word of God as the final authority."

- **Jesse Wagner**, Wagner Ministries International, Author of Brave

Daniel's book on grace settles the intense battle between the law, and grace. The battle between the legalism of works, and Jesus' finished work is over. Jesus settled it all on the cross. We are saved by grace not by anything we can do. That takes any pressure, or condemnation off of us. Daniel makes it clear that grace is God's amazing gift, now we can rest from our works in the finished work of Jesus. The battle is over.

- **Shirley Tasch**, Tasch Ministries International

In the Fight between
Religion and Relationship

GRACE WINS

DANIEL KING

Harrison House
Tulsa, Oklahoma

Unless otherwise indicated, all Scripture quotations are taken from the *New King James Version*.® Copyright © 1982 by Thomas Nelson, Inc. Used by permission. All rights reserved.

All rights reserved under International Copyright law. Contents and/or cover may not be reproduced in whole or in part in any form without the express written consent of the author.

19 18 17 16 15   5 4 3 2 1

Grace Wins

ISBN: 978-160683-875-4

Copyright © 2014 by Daniel King

Published by Harrison House Publishers

Tulsa, OK 74145

Dedication

I dedicate this book to my daughter, Katie Grace. Her graceful beauty will always remind us of God's goodness.

Thanks to Peter Youngren and my wife Jessica for making me more grace-minded. Thanks to Scott McIntyre, Susan Reidel, and Kathy Fraser for reading the manuscript and offering insights. Thanks to Luke Inberg for editing this book.

TABLE OF CONTENTS

Introduction: The Fight Is On

Round One: Weighing In
1: The Law   13
2: Desperate for Grace   19
3: Amazing Grace   25

Round Two: Jesus, the Prize Fighter
4: Jesus and the Law   39
5: Jesus and Grace   49

Round Three: Early Church Brawlers
6: Peter & Paul   57
7: The Jerusalem Council—Grace in *Acts*   65
8: The Grace Manifesto—Grace in *Romans*   71
9: Liberty for All—Grace in *Galatians*   75
10: The Grace of Good Works—Grace in *James*   83
11:Out with the Old, In with the New-Grace in *Hebrews* 95
12: The Two Mountains   103

Round Four: Going the Distance, Fighting the Confusion
13: What Grace Is Not   113
14: A License to Sin?—Grace in *Jude*   121
15: God's Judgment?   137
16: No Condemnation   145
17: The Law of Love   153
18: Grace in Your Life   161

The Final Round

Introduction: The Fight Is On

If you have given your life to Jesus Christ, you have become a recipient of the greatest gift in the history of mankind --grace.

Think about these questions:

- How did God save you?

- What brought Jesus to the earth?

- What kept Jesus on the cross as soldiers hammered nails through His hands and feet?

- Why are you forgiven of all your sins?

- Why are you going to heaven when you die?

- What empowers you to live for God here on earth?

- What is the heart of the Gospel?

- Why do good things happen to bad people?

The answer to each one of these questions is the same: Grace.

Grace will change your life.

Grace is a hot topic. Several years ago, I started hearing many preachers speak about grace. The interesting thing is that most of them disagreed with one another. Some preached on "radical grace" and others accused the "radical grace" preachers of allowing people to sin. Both sets of preachers pretended to be nice to each other, but I could tell there was a lot of underlying animosity between the two groups.

What really caught my attention was how the message of radical grace was transforming people's lives. People who discovered a revelation of grace had a fresh enthusiasm for Jesus. They were excited to talk about the Scriptures. Many of them were reading the epistles of Paul for the first time and were eager to share how their lives were being changed.

I was curious, so I decided to investigate. I started reading books about grace. The more I read, the more enthusiastic I became. I have always preached about grace, but I never really understood grace. The more I looked at it, the more I realized that grace is the most important topic in the entire Bible.

When I started studying grace, my motivation was simply to understand the issue. But to my surprise, the message changed my life. It changed my preaching. It changed my relationship with God.

Without meaning to, I had become legalistic in some of my preaching and thought patterns. I was raised in a Christian home and attended church services my whole life and over time, had picked up a lot of religious baggage. Legalism was a great weight pressing down on my shoulders, but I did not even know the burden was there until the revelation of grace began to lift it off. The message of grace made me fall in love with Jesus all over again.

As you read this book, my hope and prayer is that you will have a revelation of how great God's grace is for you—a grace that saves, that sanctifies, that sustains; a grace that is available to all and denied to none. The prophets of the Old Testament dreamed of this grace; Jesus revealed this grace; Paul preached this grace; Martin Luther rediscovered this grace, and our generation is called to manifest this grace.

Over the three years that I have been studying grace, the issue has heated up even more. Lines have been drawn. Some recently written books are *for* grace, others are *against* grace, and others still are just confused about grace. Some people are even getting kicked out of their churches because they are so excited about God's grace.

The fight is going full force. Which side will you be on? Hopefully, this book will help you choose.

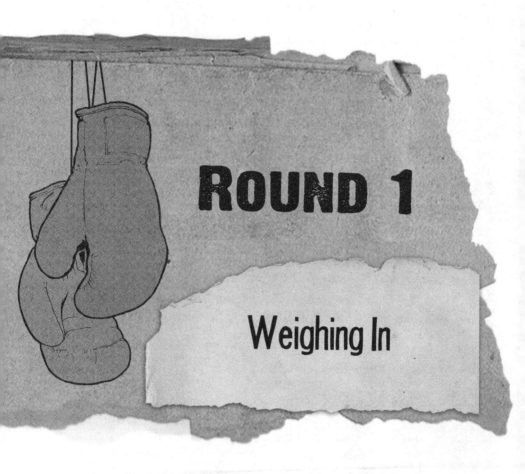

ROUND 1

Weighing In

ROUND 1

In the Church today, there is a battle over the concept of grace. Are we saved by grace? Or are we saved by keeping the Law? This epic battle is like a boxing match—and it's been going on for a few millennia. Let's peek in on the fight; the first round is about to begin.

"Let's get ready to rumble!" intones the announcer.

In the black corner stands "The Law," stern and unforgiving. The Law is like a freight train. He packs a hard punch and never backs down. Cheering for him is a formidable crowd, the best dressed and in the V.I.P. seats of the house. They all look exceptionally fine. In fact, they look like they know just how fine they appear.

In the red corner stands "Grace." Light as a butterfly, her rapid punches are swift and powerful. But who is cheering for her? A large assembly of watchers, but they don't look so pretty; a ragtag group who could have been thieves or prostitutes, or seedy leftovers from the criminal underbelly. And where they can't find a seat, they are content to observe from any space that's available.

Ding, ding! The bell sounds. The fight begins.

The Law rushes out early and starts pounding away at Grace. She attempts to dance away from his blows, but can't avoid a few devastating initial hits. First, she is double-punched with "The Ten Commandments." Then, she takes the left hook of "ritual" to the jaw. Finally, she is caught cold by "sin" and "human nature." It is not a fair fight by the looks of it.

Grace collapses to the canvas. It looks like the match is pretty much over. *Ding, ding!* Grace is saved by the bell as the round ends. But The Law is firmly in control of the bout.

Chapter One:
THE LAW

Once when I was in Pakistan, I saw a man with a flock of birds in a cage. Another man came and bought a bird. I thought he was buying the bird as a pet, but to my surprise, he immediately set the bird free. My translator explained that some people in Pakistan believe that setting a bird free is a good deed that erases a previous bad deed. They look for forgiveness through the ritual of setting birds free.

On another trip, I was in Ethiopia. The week before our team arrived in the city of Chuko, the townspeople sacrificed nine cows. They felt this religious ritual would give them favor with God.

In the nation of Nepal, the birthplace of Buddha, I visited the famous Monkey Temple that stands on a hill overlooking the city of Katmandu. I saw an old man diligently spinning prayer wheels. I witnessed a woman offering rice to a statue. I saw a monk burning incense. These individuals were trying to earn merit through human effort.

To many of us, it may seem strange to think that setting one animal free or killing another, spinning wheels, offering rice, or burning incense could affect one's status with God. But, beliefs like this are commonplace all over the world.

A typical trait of every religious tradition is the need to perform a "special deed" or a "sacred ceremony" in order to be blessed by "the gods." Muslims pray toward Mecca five times each day;

Hindus offer incense to idols; Buddhists go on long pilgrimages. And for most religions, being on "god's" good side requires a lot more than one or two simple rituals. There are whole lists of "to do's"--Buddhists follow an eight-fold path; Hindus believe in karma; Jews keep the Torah; and Muslims impose Sharia law.

Each religion asks its followers to do special deeds and good works in order to keep "God" or "the gods" happy, to avert divine or cosmic wrath, and atone for sin. Through these means, religion makes spiritual rituals the key to a successful walk with God. Spiritual rituals include things like fasting, prayer, penance, alms-giving, serving in the community, and generally doing good. As a person does all these things (and whatever other things in terms of moral laws and ethical codes that religion requires), religion promises the rewards of divine blessing and favor, with the ultimate reward being some form of "eternal life."

Unfortunately, even Christianity has been turned into such a religion. The Christian "religion" often tells people they have to perform a special task in order to be blessed by God, to be saved from sin, and to be rewarded with eternal life.

Have you ever heard these messages preached?

- Go to church or you will never make it to heaven.

- Give 10% of your income in the offering or you will be cursed.

- Meditate on Scripture or you will not have good success.

- Confess the Word or your negative talk could bring sickness on you.

All of these actions are good, but none of them are the source of God's blessing. The blessing of God comes through grace that comes from a relationship with Jesus Christ. All of these actions are the result of a grace-filled blessed life, not the cause of it.

I have heard messages on "8 Secrets to Activating the Blessing," and "The Secret of the Double-Portion Blessing," and "3 Keys to Getting a Hundred-Fold Return." The common theme of these sermons is the idea that someone must do something in order to earn favor and blessing from God. This idea is a very religious one, but it has found its way into Christian preaching, teaching, believing, and living.

Once I was in the nation of Pakistan doing a Miracle Festival. I preached that Jesus would heal the sick. After praying for the people, we asked everyone who had been healed to come up on the platform to testify. Each night, Jesus touched many Muslims. In fact, so many Muslims were healed that some of the Christians were upset. One pastor complained, "Why is Jesus healing these Muslims when some of our precious Christian believers have been sick for many years without ever being healed?"

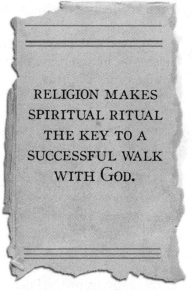

RELIGION MAKES SPIRITUAL RITUAL THE KEY TO A SUCCESSFUL WALK WITH GOD.

The answer is simple: when I announce that every person who calls on Jesus will be healed, many of the Muslims simply believe what I am saying. But, many of the Christian believers approach Jesus from a religious mindset. They are taught erroneous doctrine. Some of them believe that God uses sickness to teach us a lesson. Others believe they have to do something in order to get healed. But, the people who received their healing simply look to Jesus with faith and are healed.

This is the same situation Paul encountered with many of the Jews of His day. He says, *"They [the Jews] did not seek it [salvation] by faith, but as it were, by the works of the law. For they stumbled at that stumbling stone"* (Romans 9:32, explanations mine). The Gentiles found it easy to be saved because they simply put their faith in Jesus, while many of the Jews continued to look to the Law for their salvation.

Often, the most difficult people to help receive a miracle are those who are religious. Religious people are proud of their accomplishments. They look at all their good works and religious efforts and say, "I deserve a miracle." But none of us "deserve" a miracle. We have all sinned and fallen short of the glory of God.

Religious effort is not the key to God's wonderful blessings. Nor is it the key to a powerful ministry. The great missionary evangelist T. L. Osborn came to my house once when twenty-seven young evangelists had flown in from different parts of the world to meet with him and learn from his lifetime experience of crusade evangelism. For three hours, he shared stories and insights from years of ministry.

At one point, a young preacher asked Dr. Osborn the question: "Is there a price to be paid to be in the healing ministry?" The young man wanted to discover how much prayer, fasting, and Bible reading it would take to be successful in ministry.

"Yes, there is a very high price to be paid," Dr. Osborn responded, but immediately continued: "Jesus paid it all on the cross."

In one sentence, Dr. Osborn completely changed my theology. Early in my ministry, I desperately wanted to see miracles happen when I preached. So I spent lots of time fasting and praying. But as I gained more experience, I realized that no matter how much I fasted, I would never be able to heal someone through my own effort. By myself, I couldn't heal a migraine, let alone cancer or HIV.

Healings, miracles, salvations, the anointing of God, and a powerful ministry have never been the fruit of religious effort. These things only happen because of what Jesus did on the cross. Dr. Osborn's insight took the responsibility for miracles off my own efforts and put the responsibility directly on Jesus. What a relief!

But if religious effort is not the key to receiving a miracle or being an anointed minister, why is it that many count so much on religious effort? Why has this happened? Why have many Christians fallen into this trap? Why has so much theology been skewed, so much teaching been spoiled, and so much effort been wasted? How many souls have been imperiled by these religious notions?

The answer to these questions is because man wants to be right with God. Only a small percentage of the population of the globe disputes the existence of God. Most of the world believes in some form of divinity. Where there is belief in divinity, there is a sense that our lives are affected by that power. Mankind wants to be on the good side of whatever divinity it believes in. This is the natural desire, the core of religion--the ways and means of being on the good side of the divine. So much for mankind in general, but what about Christians specifically? Why has our faith become so religious for so many people? Maybe it is because many Christians lack a personal revelation of God's grace. Christians who lack a revelation of God's grace will exalt good works, spiritual disciplines, morality, and will look to religious traditions to guide them in their relationship and walk with God.

Besides that, in the Old Testament, God saw fit to reveal Himself through a code of laws. The Law that is contained in the Hebrew Scriptures is recognized as the Word of God, as a revelation of God to mankind. This Law is full of moral teachings, ethical codes, ritualistic requirements, and instructions for almost every area of life. In total, it includes 445 laws. Part of the construction of the Law included assurances that you would be blessed if you did what the Law said, and cursed if you failed to keep it. Christians fall back on an old revelation of God in an attempt to be right with Him.

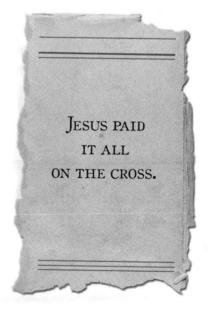

JESUS PAID
IT ALL
ON THE CROSS.

The problem with this old revelation is that it is old, worn out, and weak. No man shall be justified by the works of the Law.

How can you escape the trap of religion? How can you be established in a joyful faith in Christ? Let's look at some people and the stories of how they discovered new joy, new life, and new enthusiasm for God through a revelation of His grace.

Chapter Two:

DESPERATE FOR GRACE

When compared to all of the other religions in the world, true Christianity stands unique. The main difference is that other religions offer a system of earning merit through human works, while Christianity relies solely upon unearned divine grace. Yet, true Christianity is not always easy to find. Over the ages, the Christian religion has imposed just as many rules as any other belief system.

The Story of Martin Luther

During the Middle Ages, the view of the church (in this case, the Roman Catholic Church) was that grace was a treasure that was managed and dispensed by the church and its organization. Believers did not inherently receive grace as believers, but priests taught that if one gave money to the church, prayed enough, or did enough good works, one could earn grace. Grace was the result of religious effort and spiritual discipline. It was into this cultural understanding of grace that Martin Luther was born.

As a young man, Luther was almost struck by a bolt of lightning. The terror caused by this incident led him to change his vocation. He chose to become a monk, rather than the lawyer his father had hoped he would be. Luther was scared of God, and becoming a monk was part of a quest to become holy, pleasing to God, and a recipient of His grace.

Luther tried every means of grace that the Roman Catholic Church offered: sacraments, indulgences, attending mass, confession of sins to a priest, pilgrimages, and the intercession of the saints. Yet despite his efforts, he continually struggled with the fact that he fell short of God's standard of holiness. He suffered from an overwhelming sense of sinfulness.

Martin Luther wrote, "If ever a monk could get to heaven through monastic discipline, I was that monk. And yet my conscience would not give me certainty. I always doubted and said, 'You didn't do that right. You weren't contrite enough. You left that out of your confession.' The more I tried to remedy an uncertain, weak, and troubled conscience with human traditions, the more I daily found it more uncertain, weak, and troubled."

Depression set in, "Anfectungen" as Luther called it, or "spiritual depression." Extremely aware of God's holiness, and yet at the same time, understanding that he was completely unable to appease God's sense of justice with his own religious works and self-discipline, Luther was left to ponder his God in the image of an angry, vindictive judge.

One story of how he tried to resolve the spiritual depression illustrates the futile nature of trying to earn salvation through human works. During a visit to Rome, Luther visited many of the great churches. It is said that when he visited each church, he got down on his knees and religiously kissed each step that led to the church door. Such actions arose from Luther's desperate desire to please God.

It was during this time that Luther studied the epistles of Paul. As he studied Romans and Galatians, He became disturbed by the church's emphasis on keeping religious rules. He read in Romans 3:28, *"a man is justified by faith apart from the deeds of the law."* As he continued to read, Luther received the revelation that people are saved by faith alone (*sola fide*) and by grace alone (*sola gratia*).

Because of his new understanding of grace, Luther began to challenge the religious status quo, writing *The Ninety-Five Theses* and nailing them to the door of the cathedral in Wittenberg. Luther's new theology became the basis of the Protestant Reformation. The core of this theology was that justification and salvation, that is, the place of being made right with God and saved from the penalties of sin, comes through God's grace, not from one's own works. Grace is a free gift from God; it is not earned, purchased or administered by the church.

For Luther, discovering grace was the end of a long stormy voyage, and it opened up a whole new spiritual life for him.

The Sale of "Indulgences"

Luther was not the only one desperate to please God. There were many others like him who hoped to somehow be right with God, and they embraced the means that the church had to offer. One significant means was the purchase of an "indulgence."

The theological reasoning behind the sale of indulgences was that the church had a large store of grace available. This grace came from the prayers of the saints. Since the church had so much grace available, they were able to dispense it at will in exchange for cold, hard cash. This proved to be attractive to illiterate, uneducated peasants across Europe. Some priests taught that people and their loved ones who were destined for purgatory, even hell, could change their destination and get on the fast-track to heaven through the purchase of indulgences.

FOR LUTHER, DISCOVERING GRACE WAS THE END OF A LONG STORMY VOYAGE.

John Tetzel was among those who preached about and sold indulgences. A saying famously attributed to him goes like this: "As soon as a coin in the coffer rings, the soul from purgatory springs." For people wanting grace at any cost, it was not a hard sell and people flocked to Tetzel in order to purchase his indulgences.

Luther, who observed this, witnessed the hardship of the people who sacrificed everything in order to purchase an indulgence. Such was the desire for grace!

Peter Rodriguez's Story

Luther and the faithful of the Middle Ages were desperate for grace. Their stories are still echoed in the lives of Christian believers today.

My friend, Peter Rodriguez, grew up in a denomination that was extremely legalistic. His church had rules about everything-- rules about clothing, rules about baptism, rules that a woman could not cut her hair, wear makeup, or curl her eyelashes, rules forbidding wedding rings. They taught that their church was the only way to get to heaven. If a church member did not follow the constitution and rules of the church, they were ostracized from fellowship.

Peter never knew if he was really saved. He felt bound up in religion and held hostage to rules made up by men. He felt empty because he always fell short of expectations. He was caught in the rat race of legalism. He always had to outdo his last good act. He felt condemned if he so much as missed a church service. He usually felt all-around guilty about himself and his lifestyle.

Peter and his wife were involved in leading music at their church, but they always sensed they were not quite good enough to be on the platform. Peter's wife was criticized for cutting her hair. They were labeled as rebellious.

Their church leaders were brutal on the laity. They kept pushing people to do more and more. The leaders imposed strict standards on their members, even though the leaders themselves were unable to keep all the rules. Image was more important than love. One church leader brutally beat his son for going to the movie theater. Other leaders preached strong sermons about holiness, but were caught sexually abusing children. Repeatedly, the congregation heard that God was angry and disapproving.

Today, many of Peter's friends and others he grew up with in church are no longer serving God. They listened to the condemning legalistic preaching in his church and figured, "If I am condemned anyway, I might as well do something really bad." Many of them fell into drug and alcohol addiction, sexual perversity, and living a life of sin.

Eventually, Peter and his wife both tumbled into severe depression. They were unable to handle the condemnation and judgment that came from other members of their church. They sought professional counseling, but what really set them free was a Bible study. At a home group, they started to hear about God's grace. Slowly, the message of grace released them from the trap of legalism.

Peter says, "It was hard for me to recognize grace. I had a difficult time knowing that God loved me. But slowly I discovered that in spite of who I am, God still blesses me. He taught me to receive His love. Little by little, God peeled away the distortion and revealed Himself to me. I saw that God is a God of grace. Now I know that He cares for me."

He continues, "Grace, like a tsunami wave without warning, crossed high walls of my legalism. It flooded my deepest inferior valleys that harbored my psychological, physical, and spiritual tragedies. It overwhelmed me. It keeps seeing me for what I can be and not for what I am. How could I not have noticed grace before?"

Now, Peter and his wife Lorena are serving the Lord wholeheartedly. They had to move across the country to escape the negative influence of their old church. God opened up doors for them to minister to other people. Most importantly of all, today they are walking in the freedom of God's grace.

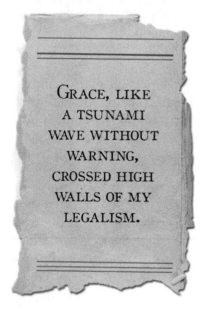

GRACE, LIKE A TSUNAMI WAVE WITHOUT WARNING, CROSSED HIGH WALLS OF MY LEGALISM.

Discovering Grace

Luther, Rodriguez, and so many others, past and present, are hungry for God's grace. So many need to know the love of God! People need to hear the good, joyful news of salvation, not be given a list of powerless rules. It is so important that we have a revelation of God's grace.

What is your story? Have you ever felt trapped by legalistic religion? Have religious rules frustrated you? Do you ever feel like you are going to church out of rote habit instead of because church refreshes you? Do you ever wonder if there is something more to Christianity? If you answered "Yes" to any of these questions, keep reading. You are about to discover God's amazing grace.

Chapter Three:
AMAZING GRACE

Have you ever been amazed? A Sequoia tree—the largest living thing on our planet—amazing! The sheer volume of water pouring over Niagara Falls—amazing! The Great Wall of China, stretching for hundreds and hundreds of miles over rugged terrain—amazing! Buzz Aldrin and Neil Armstrong stepping onto the moon—amazing! Roger Bannister running the first four-minute mile—amazing! A man falling in love with a woman—amazing! There are many amazing things in this world, but the most amazing thing of all is God's grace.

John Newton, "an infidel and a libertine" as he would call himself, was among other things, a slave trader. Newton jammed 600 slaves into the bowels of his ship. They were chained together and forced to stand for the two-month voyage from Africa to the New World. Up to 20% of the slaves died en route due to the inhumane conditions on the ship. In 1748, Newton left the shores of Sierra Leone with a ship full of slaves and was engulfed in a massive storm. In the midst of the tempest and afraid for his life, Newton cried out to God to "save his wretched soul!" The storm did not overwhelm the vessel, and Newton survived to sail another day.

This conversion experience set Newton on a journey that would eventually lead him to become a clergyman, a preacher of the Gospel, and an abolitionist (he would be instrumental in helping William Wilberforce abolish the slave trade in England). Newton's real life encounter with God's grace inspired him to pen the words of the famous hymn, "Amazing Grace:"

Amazing grace! How sweet the sound
That saved a wretch like me!
I once was lost, but now am found,
Was blind, but now I see.

But what's so amazing about grace? What makes anything amazing? It's the seeming impossibility of a thing that amazes. The redwood, the roaring falls, walking on the moon, overcoming physical handicaps, love—it's the seeming impossibility of these things that make us gape and wonder. If these things make us think of the impossible, maybe it's because they are just shadows and types of the seeming impossibility of the grace of God.

What Is Grace?

What is grace? The English word "grace" comes from the Latin word *gratia*, which means "pleasing or thankful." The Greek word for grace, found throughout the New Testament, is *charis*. The picture this word provides is that of a ruler who having conquered a rebellious people, allows them to live despite their opposition. "Charm" is another aspect of the meaning of this beautiful word.

In times past, the subjects of a king would refer to him as "Your Grace." When the credit card company gives you extra time to pay your bill, they call it a "grace period." A beautifully coordinated dancer is called "graceful." When a politician falls from favor because of a mistake, we say they are "dis-graced."

Grace is often referred to as the unmerited favor of God. The dictionary says grace is the condition or fact of being favored by someone. Strong's Concordance says that grace is the divine influence upon the heart and its reflection in life. Grace has been defined as God's unmerited, undeserved, unearned favor, blessing, and ability.

The word "grace" has even been transformed into an acronym--G.R.A.C.E., or God's Riches At Christ's Expense. Because of Christ's sacrifice on the cross, we experience all of God's blessings:

His mercy, His forgiveness, His help, His resources, and His love. All these things have been given to us freely. Grace is a one-word definition of salvation. Grace is God doing for us what we could not do for ourselves. Grace is God providing for us what we could not provide. Grace is God being what we could not be.

What Does Grace Do for You?

Look at all the things grace does for you. Because of grace...

...You are called. *"[He] has saved us and called us with a holy calling, not according to our works, but according to His own purpose and grace which was given to us in Christ Jesus before time began"* (2 Timothy 1:9).

...You believe. *"[Apollos] greatly helped those who had believed through grace"* (Acts 18:27).

...You are saved. *"By grace you have been saved"* (Ephesians 2:5). *"For the grace of God that brings salvation has appeared to all men"* (Titus 2:11).

...You are justified. *"Being justified freely by His grace through the redemption that is in Christ Jesus"* (Romans 3:24).

...You are accepted by God. *"The glory of His grace, by which He made us accepted in the Beloved"* (Ephesians 1:6).

...Your sins are forgiven. *"In Him we have redemption through His blood, the forgiveness of sins, according to the riches of His grace"* (Ephesians 1:7).

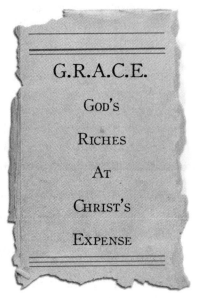

G.R.A.C.E.

GOD'S

RICHES

AT

CHRIST'S

EXPENSE

…You overcome sin. *"For sin shall not have dominion over you, for you are not under law but under grace"* (Romans 6:14).

…You overcome every weakness. *"And He said to me, 'My grace is sufficient for you, for My strength is made perfect in weakness'"* (2 Corinthians 12:9).

…You are sanctified. *"By that will we have been sanctified through the offering of the body of Jesus Christ once for all"* (Hebrews 10:10).

…You are empowered to live for God. *"Let us have grace, by which we may serve God acceptably with reverence and godly fear"* (Hebrews 12:28).

…You learn how to live a holy life. *"[Grace teaches] us that, denying ungodliness and worldly lusts, we should live soberly, righteously, and godly in the present age, looking for the blessed hope and glorious appearing of our great God and Savior Jesus Christ"* (Titus 2:11-13).

…You receive miracles. *"Therefore they stayed there a long time, speaking boldly in the Lord, who was bearing witness to the word of His grace, granting signs and wonders to be done by their hands"* (Acts 14:3).

…You have a spiritual gift. *"Having then gifts differing according to the grace that is given to us, let us use them: if prophecy, let us prophesy in proportion to our faith; or ministry, let us use it in our ministering; he who teaches, in teaching; he who exhorts, in exhortation; he who gives, with liberality; he who leads, with diligence; he who shows mercy, with cheerfulness"* (Romans 12:6-8).

…You have hope. *"Now may our Lord Jesus Christ Himself, and our God and Father, who has loved us and given us everlasting consolation and good hope by grace, comfort your hearts and establish you in every good word and work"* (2 Thessalonians 2:16-17).

…You can be thankful. *"For all things are for your sakes, that grace, having spread through the many, may cause thanksgiving to abound to the glory of God"* (2 Corinthians 4:15).

…You have an inheritance. *"So now, brethren, I commend you to God and to the word of His grace, which is able to build you up and give you an inheritance among all those who are sanctified"* (Acts 20:32).

…You have eternal life. *"So grace might reign through righteousness to eternal life through Jesus Christ our Lord"* (Romans 5:20).

…You are an heir with Christ *"By His grace we should become heirs according to the hope of eternal life"* (Titus 3:7).

…You reign with Christ. *"For if by the one man's offense death reigned through the one, much more those who receive abundance of grace and of the gift of righteousness will reign in life through the One, Jesus Christ"* (Romans 5:17).

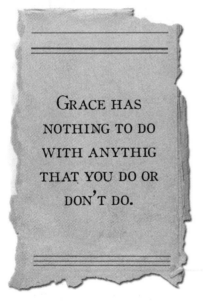

GRACE HAS NOTHING TO DO WITH ANYTHIG THAT YOU DO OR DON'T DO.

God's grace does a lot for you. It is rich grace, abundant grace, many-sided grace. Are you amazed yet?

Where Does All This Grace Come From?

How does this grace become available to you? Is it because of how hard you pray, how much you believe, how sinless you are or how much good you do? No. Grace has nothing to do with anything that you do or don't do. Grace is all about what only God can do. The Son of God came into our world as Jesus Christ, and grace and truth came with Him. In what ways can you experience the grace of God in His Son?

1. Forgiveness in Jesus

The power of grace is its ability to overcome sin. No sin in your life is bigger than God's mercy and grace. No sin is bigger than Jesus Christ's sacrifice for sin. Look at these amazing verses:

"Your sins are forgiven" (Matthew 9:2).

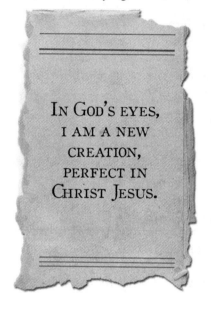

IN GOD'S EYES, I AM A NEW CREATION, PERFECT IN CHRIST JESUS.

"Whoever believes in [Jesus] will receive remission of sins" (Acts 10:43).

"Through this Man is preached to you the forgiveness of sins" (Acts 13:38).

"In [Jesus] we have redemption through His blood, the forgiveness of sins, according to the riches of His grace" (Ephesians 1:7).

"God in Christ forgave you" (Ephesians 4:32).

"We have redemption through [Jesus'] blood, the forgiveness of sins" (Colossians 1:14).

"Your sins are forgiven you for His name's sake" (1 John 2:12).

Are you getting the message? Your sins are forgiven!

Martin Luther wrote, "Either sin is with you, lying on your shoulders, or it is lying on Christ, the Lamb of God. Now if it is lying on your back, you are lost; but if it is resting on Christ, you are free, and you will be saved. Now choose what you want." Fred Price said, "You're not a sinner saved by grace. You're either a sinner or you're saved by grace. You can't be both."

Are you a sinner? Your actions, thoughts, and motives are often contrary to God's laws. Yet in God's eyes, you are a new creation, perfect in Christ Jesus. How can this be? The answer is grace.

2. Salvation in Jesus

Everyone has sinned and the penalty for sin is death. But Jesus died on the cross to pay the penalty for our sins. Through His work on the cross, we can be saved.

Even Old Testament saints will be in heaven because of their faith in Jesus. Jesus proclaimed, *"I am the way, the truth, and the life. No one comes to the Father except through Me"* (John 14:6). He also told the Jews, *"Your father Abraham rejoiced to see My day, and he saw it and was glad"* (John 8:56).

After Jesus died on the cross, those who during Old Testament times trusted God's promises about the coming Savior, were retroactively saved by faith under the terms of the New Covenant. This is what was promised in Jeremiah 31:31-33, *"Behold, the days are coming, says the LORD, when I will make a new covenant with the house of Israel and with the house of Judah--not according to the covenant that I made with their fathers in the day that I took them by the hand to lead them out of the land of Egypt, My covenant which they broke, though I was a husband to them, says the LORD. But this is the covenant that I will make with the house of Israel after those days, says the LORD: I will put My law in their minds, and write it on their hearts; and I will be their God, and they shall be My people."*

3. Victory in Jesus

As believers, we are not fighting for victory, we are fighting from a position of victory. Jesus won the victory on the cross; everything else is just celebration. As a believer in Jesus, you can never be more victorious than you are right now.

"Yet in all these things we are more than conquerors through Him who loved us" (Romans 8:37).

"But thanks be to God, who gives us the victory through our Lord Jesus Christ" (1 Corinthians 15:57).

"Now thanks be to God who always leads us in triumph in Christ" (2 Corinthians 2:14).

4. Blessing in Jesus

GOD HAS BLESSED US WITH EVERY SPIRITUAL BLESSING.

Do you want to be blessed? Do you desire to live a life of abundance? Have you been searching for a way to be more blessed than you are right now? In Exodus 19:5, God promises, *"If you obey my commands, you will be blessed."* But in the New Testament, God replaced this conditional blessing with an unconditional blessing.

How often do we ask God for blessings that are already ours in Christ? Paul wrote in Ephesians 1:3, *"Blessed be the God and Father of our Lord Jesus Christ, who has blessed us with every spiritual blessing."* Did you read that? You have been blessed with every spiritual blessing. There is nothing God is going to do for you that He has not already done.

According to Paul, you do not need to be blessed. You *are* blessed with every spiritual blessing. What more do you need? You are blessed with healing. You are blessed with salvation. You are blessed with prosperity. You are blessed in every way!

Sometimes we struggle and strain to get blessed without realizing that we are already blessed. It is like trying to get into a car you are already sitting in. People who try to get blessed are like a little girl who visited the Statue of Liberty in New York City. During her visit, she noticed a guard standing nearby.

"I want to buy it," said the girl, pointing at the colossal statue.

"How much do you have?" asked the guard.

"Twenty-five cents," replied the girl.

"Well, you need to understand three things" the guard explained. "First, twenty-five cents is not enough to purchase the statue, in fact, even if you had millions of dollars it would not be enough. Second, the Statue of Liberty is not for sale. And third, if you are an American citizen, you already own it!"

It's the same way with God's blessing. If you are trying to get blessed, there are three things you need to understand. First, you do not have enough money to purchase the blessing of God. Second, the blessing of God is not for sale. Third, if you are a Christian, you are already blessed!

As Jesus died on the cross, He proclaimed, "It is finished!" You don't need to do anything more in order to be blessed. You just need to understand the fullness of what Jesus accomplished on the cross. You don't need to sacrifice cows, say ritualistic prayers, or go on a long pilgrimage. All you have to say is "Thank you, Jesus!"

Matthew Barnett tweeted: "The saying, 'You get what you pay for' should be replaced by, 'We get what Jesus paid for.'"

5. Rest in Jesus

When God made a covenant with Abraham in Genesis chapter 15, He actually put Abraham to sleep and stood in for him at the covenant ceremony. God fulfilled both His side of the covenant and Abraham's side of the covenant. Why? Because there was no way Abraham could have fulfilled his part of the bargain. Abraham rested and God did everything.

In the same way, we should rest in what Jesus has already done for us. With Jesus, there is no straining and striving. Jesus says, "My yoke is easy and My burden is light" (Matthew 11:30).

When Jesus ascended back into heaven, He sat down at the right side of His Father (Hebrews 8:1). Why did Jesus sit down? Because all the work was finished. So, if Jesus is sitting down, why are we struggling and straining to accomplish something that is already done? Our role is to rest in what Jesus has accomplished.

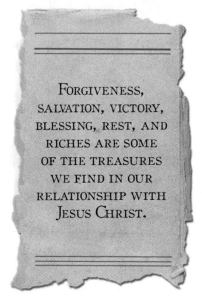

FORGIVENESS, SALVATION, VICTORY, BLESSING, REST, AND RICHES ARE SOME OF THE TREASURES WE FIND IN OUR RELATIONSHIP WITH JESUS CHRIST.

Recently, my vehicle needed an oil change, but the place where I got my maintenance closed at five o'clock. I was stuck in traffic, so I was zooming in and out of different lanes, cutting people off and running yellow lights in an effort to get to the shop before it closed. I was under so much stress and strain. I picked up my cell phone and called my wife Jessica and she said, "Oh, I went in and got the oil changed last week." Suddenly, all my worry was gone so I leisurely took my time driving home. Why? Because the work was finished; it was done.

"For he who has entered His rest has himself also ceased from his works as God did from His. Let us therefore be diligent to enter that rest." (Hebrews 4:10-11).

6. Riches in Jesus

In the ages to come, God will reveal all the riches of His grace. For all eternity, you will be reigning with Christ. What a rich future we look forward to! Through Jesus, we walk in abundance, both in this life and the life to come.

"When we were dead in trespasses, [He] made us alive together with Christ (by grace you have been saved), and raised us up together, and made us sit together in the heavenly places in Christ Jesus, that in the ages to come He might show the exceeding riches of His grace in His kindness toward us in Christ Jesus" (Ephesians 2:5-7).

Grace is amazing! But it is only as we understand God's grace and abandon our misplaced trust in religious rituals and trust in Christ alone, that we will come to understand and experience just how amazing grace really is.

Forgiveness, salvation, victory, blessing, rest, and riches are some of the treasures we find in our relationship with Jesus Christ. But what about all the rules and regulations of religion? Can Jesus set us free from those? Keep reading to find out.

ROUND 2

Jesus, the Prize Fighter

ROUND 2

The short breather has done Grace a world of good. Coach Jesus has been in her corner, encouraging her, giving her a pep talk, handing out the ice packs, and making sure Grace's shoulders aren't cramping.

Ding, ding! The second round gets underway.

Again, The Law tries to dominate. He throws everything at Grace, hoping to give her the bum's rush. Left-hooks, jabs, uppercuts, straight rights, combinations, haymakers, even a kidney shot…The Law is a real brawler. But Grace manages to dance around, keep her distance, and parry the glancing blows that happen to connect.

In the final seconds of the round, Jesus spreads wide His arms and shouts, "Get 'em, Grace!" Grace delivers a hard liver shot with a devastating effect.

The Law staggers and falls. The second round ends with The Law on his knees.

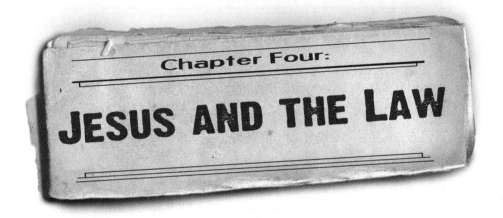

Chapter Four:
JESUS AND THE LAW

I graduated from a conservative Christian university. Rules and standards of conduct were an extremely important part of the university's culture. At the beginning of the year, every student was required to sign an "Honor Code." The students were then expected to stick to the honor code or suffer expulsion.

The rules at my school were originally instituted back in the 1960's when many young people were rebelling against authority. At that time, the university was known as a beacon of light because of the moral conduct and behavior it required and promoted. But good behavior and moral conduct were not the only requirements. Male students were forbidden to wear beards or blue jeans; female students had to wear skirts to class and the cafeteria. Curfew was strictly enforced. Drinking and dancing were not allowed.

By the time I arrived in 1998, much of the justification for the rules had worn thin. Students chaffed under the restrictions. Every year the students would petition to wear blue jeans, and every year they were denied. When the students asked why they could not wear blue jeans, they were told, "Because that's the rule."

Unfortunately, my experience is not an isolated exception; for too many, it's been the rule. In churches and in Christian education settings, so often the core message of God's Word, grace, is ignored.

A pastor once asked me on the phone: "Are you one of those grace preachers?"

I could hear the antagonism in his tone. I replied, "Why do you ask?"

"I'm sick and tired of all of these grace preachers telling people they can sin."

"I definitely don't encourage people to sin," I exclaimed, "but I do preach about grace. I think we all need God's grace in order to be saved."

"Well, when you come to my church, you can preach on anything God leads you to preach on, just do not talk about grace."

As I hung up the phone, I thought, *It is a sad day when a preacher is asked to ignore the core message of the New Testament.*

Why was I thinking this way? Ask yourself: Without grace, what is left in the Bible worth preaching about? Without grace, what does the Bible become?

Without grace, the Bible becomes more or less just a grand set of rules and regulations. Without grace, all we are left with is the Law.

How Did Jesus Handle the Law?

At first glance, Jesus should have loved the Pharisees. They were trying to live holy lives, and they were trying to get other people to live holy lives too. They were faithful to pray. They were givers, tithing religiously. They were evangelists, working hard to make converts. They seemed to be doing everything right. But Jesus couldn't stand them, and He adamantly detested their focus on the Law.

Look at the intensity with which Jesus chastises the Pharisees in Matthew 23:1-38. He says *"Woe to you"* eight times to the

Pharisees. Six times He calls them *"hypocrites"* because while they taught the Law, they did not do it themselves. Five times He calls them *"blind guides"* or *"blind fools."* Jesus ridicules their focus on the Law, calling it *"straining out a gnat and swallowing a camel."* He says they are like a cup that is clean on the outside but filthy on the inside. He likens them to a whitewashed tomb, outwardly beautiful, but inside full of dead men's bones. He names them *"serpents and a brood of vipers."* Jesus condemned the Pharisees and teachers of the Law in the strongest terms possible: *"How can you escape the condemnation of hell"* (Matthew 28:33). After all these insults, is it any wonder the Pharisees wanted to crucify Jesus?

But wanting Jesus dead was only adding more fuel to the flames of His rebukes. At one point He said to them, *"Did not Moses give you the Law, and yet none of you carries out the Law? Why do you seek to kill Me?"* (John 7:19). One of the Ten Commandants is, "Thou shalt not kill." The very ones accusing Jesus of breaking the Law were themselves breaking the Law by wanting to kill Him.

In every encounter with them, Jesus showed the teachers of the Law and the Pharisees the utter ridiculousness of their efforts to keep the Law. He told the people, *"Unless your righteousness exceeds the righteousness of the scribes and Pharisees, you will by no means enter the kingdom of heaven"* (Matthew 5:20). Jesus' listeners would instantly have despaired of hope. If they had to be more holy than the holiest among them, how could anyone ever enter heaven?

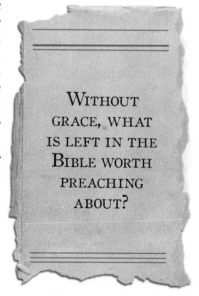

WITHOUT GRACE, WHAT IS LEFT IN THE BIBLE WORTH PREACHING ABOUT?

Jesus Intensified The Law.

If the complexities of keeping the Pharisaical Law weren't hard enough, Jesus intensified the Law beyond even the most religiously inclined person's capacity to keep it. The Old Testament set an extremely high standard for how to live and act, but Jesus raised the bar higher still by revealing that people will be judged for more than just their actions. Let's look at how Jesus made the Law even harder to keep.

1. Anger equals murder. *"You have heard that it was said to those of old, 'You shall not murder, and whoever murders will be in danger of the judgment.' But I say to you that whoever is angry with his brother without a cause shall be in danger of the judgment. And whoever says to his brother, 'Raca!' shall be in danger of the council. But whoever says, 'You fool!' shall be in danger of hell fire"* (Matthew 5:21-22).

Have you ever been angry and found out that it was unjustified?

2. Lust equals adultery. *"You have heard that it was said to those of old, 'You shall not commit adultery.' But I say to you that whoever looks at a woman to lust for her has already committed adultery with her in his heart"* (Matthew 5:27-28).

Most men would admit to checking out a woman on occasion.

3. If part of your body causes you to sin, it must be punished. *"If your right eye causes you to sin, pluck it out and cast it from you; for it is more profitable for you that one of your members perish, than for your whole body to be cast into hell. And if your right hand causes you to sin, cut it off and cast it from you; for it is more profitable for you that one of your members perish, than for your whole body to be cast into hell"* (Matthew 5:29-30).

If we truly obeyed these verses, there would be a lot of Christians without eyes and hands!

If You Could Keep the Entire Law, You Would be an Amazing Human Being.

Jesus made the Law, as comprehensive as it was, even more all-encompassing. Not only are you required to be perfect in your outward behavior, but you also have to be perfect in your thoughts, intentions, and motives. Jesus commands, *"Be perfect, just as your Father in heaven is perfect"* (Matthew 5:48). This word "perfect" is the Greek word *teleios* meaning nothing lacking, complete, perfect. How can anyone ever fulfill this command?

"Whoever therefore breaks one of the least of these commandments, and teaches men so, shall be called least in the kingdom of heaven; but whoever does and teaches them, he shall be called great in the kingdom of heaven" (Matthew 5:19). If you could be perfect,

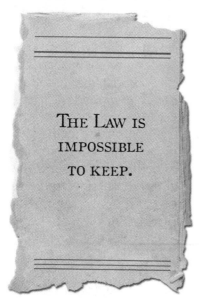

THE LAW IS IMPOSSIBLE TO KEEP.

if you could keep the whole Law, you would be great. Better than great even, you would be amazing! Why? Because the Law is impossible to keep. If you break even one of the laws, you might as well have broken every single one of them: *"For whoever shall keep the whole law and yet stumble in one point, he is guilty of all"* (James 2:10). Once you decide to try to be righteous by keeping part of the Law, you have to keep the rest of the Law too—it's an all or nothing venture.

Many people think they can pick and choose what parts of the Law to obey. The book of Leviticus (part of the Law of Moses) tells us that it is wrong to eat pork, shrimp or lobster, and that it is wrong to wear poly-blend cotton, work on the Sabbath, charge interest, or shave your beard. Also, every man must be circumcised, and

EVERYONE PICKS AND CHOOSES THE RULES THEY WANT TO KEEP.

women must not cut their hair. Do you know anyone who follows all these laws?

The rule that most frustrated the young men at my university was a ban on facial hair. Student leaders would roam the campus and if they saw a male student with the beginnings of a beard, they would force him to go back to the dorms to shave. One day, a chapel speaker was preaching about maintaining standards of holiness. He had us turn in our Bibles to Leviticus 19:28. He used the verse to preach about how bad it is to get a tattoo. As we read the verse he was preaching from, my eyes wandered to the verse right above which forbids the Israelites to shave their beards. I remember being struck by the fact that the school chose to follow some verses from the Law while rejecting other verses.

Altogether, the Law encompasses the Ten Commandments and various other civil, moral, dietary, and sacrificial laws. No one manages to keep all of these laws. Some choose to only follow the Ten Commandments. Others choose to ignore the dietary laws, but they follow the moral laws. Animal sacrifices are decidedly outdated. Everyone picks and chooses the rules they want to keep.

So, which sins are "acceptable" and which sins are "unacceptable?" Many point to the sins of others as being horrible, but they excuse their own sins. They say, "My own sins deserve grace, but the sin of that man (pointing a finger) are beyond the pale," or "It is forgivable for me to lie sometimes, but for a homosexual to engage in unnatural acts with his body is really sinful." Matthew Barnett tweeted, "People who make a list of what sins are worse than others rarely have theirs in the Top Ten."

Look at what Paul said, *"Do you not know that the unrighteous will not inherit the kingdom of God? Do not be deceived. Neither fornicators, nor idolaters, nor adulterers, nor homosexuals, nor sodomites, nor thieves, nor covetous, nor drunkards, nor revilers, nor extortioners will inherit the kingdom of God"* (1 Corinthians 6:9-10). According to this verse, adultery and coveting my neighbor's new car are just as wrong as homosexuality.

It is a waste of time to dispute about which parts of the Law are to be obeyed: *"But avoid foolish disputes, genealogies, contentions, and strivings about the law; for they are unprofitable and useless"* (Titus 3:9). In the end, a little of the Law is as powerful as the whole Law. As Paul said, *"A little leaven leavens the whole lump"* (Galatians 5:9). If you put a little bit of yeast into your dough, it will affect the entire loaf. In the same way, a little Law has a big impact on your salvation. Even if you keep ninety-nine out of one hundred laws, by breaking one, you are guilty of breaking all of them. Either you are perfectly perfect in every requirement of the Law, or you need a Savior.

Jesus Fulfilled the Law

For all that Jesus rebuked the Pharisees for their focus on the Law, and for all that He intensified it, Jesus took the Law seriously. In His famous Sermon on the Mount Jesus said: *"Do not think that I came to destroy the Law or the Prophets. I did not come to destroy but to fulfill. For assuredly, I say to you, till heaven and earth pass away, one jot or one tittle will by no means pass from the law till all is fulfilled"* (Matthew 7:17-18).

The important part of this verse is that Jesus fulfilled the Law, not that the Law would never pass away. In all of history, Jesus is the only man who completely kept both the detail (the outward behavioral requirements) and the spirit (the inward requirements regarding our intentions and motivations) of the Law. And because Jesus fulfilled the Law, the Law is not needed anymore. Look at what the Apostle Paul says: *"For Christ is the end of the law for righteousness to everyone who believes. For Moses writes about the righteousness which is of the law, The man who does those things shall live by them* (Romans 10:4-5). Christ is the end of the Law. The Law continues to exist, but those who have put their trust in Christ are dead to it.

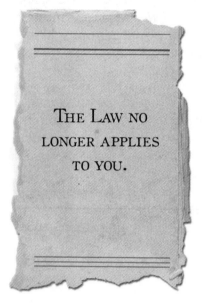

THE LAW NO LONGER APPLIES TO YOU.

Jesus fulfilled the Law, and grace is the new reality for those who put their trust in Him. The Law gets thrown out. This is not always easy to grasp. One pastor told me, "We need to have one foot in the Old Testament and one foot in the New Testament. We need to keep a balance between Law and grace." Many say you have to balance grace by teaching people to keep the Law. But Paul calls this *"a different Gospel"* (Galatians 1:6).

In 2 Kings 4:38-40, Elisha the prophet asked his protégés to cook a pot of stew. One young man accidentally put a poisonous wild gourd in the pot. Because there was "death" in the pot, the prophets were not able to eat. A little bit of poison made all the good food inedible. Many preachers do the same thing today by trying to mix the gospel of grace with the poison of legalism.

Grace and works are like oil and water, they do not mix. *"And if by grace, then it is no longer of works; otherwise grace is no longer grace. But if it is of works, it is no longer grace; otherwise work is no longer work"* (Romans 11:6). If even a little bit of human goodness is required for salvation, then salvation ceases to be the work of God alone. Andy Stanley says, "Grace plus anything is anything but grace." Paul reveals

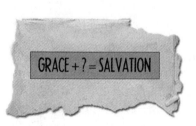

GRACE + ? = SALVATION

that salvation comes only by grace, from the beginning to the end, or salvation is not by grace at all. If righteousness comes through our works, then Jesus died for nothing. If righteousness comes through our obedience, then Jesus only paid part of the price.

Once you accept the concept of grace, you can't fit your life into the old paradigm of trying to keep the Law. As Jesus said, *"You can't put new wine in old wineskins"* (Matthew 9:17). As soon as you try to balance grace and the Law, you render grace null and void. If even a little bit of religious work is required for salvation, then salvation stops being the work of God and His grace. If you are counting on even one Law to make you righteous, then you are not trusting the work of Christ at all, but rather the Law.

My grandfather did not file a tax return with the IRS this year. Normally, the IRS would launch an investigation and prosecute him for failing to pay his taxes, but they did nothing to my grandfather. Why? For one simple reason: my grandfather is dead. The law no longer applies to him.

The Law no longer applies to you. It is time for you to start walking in the grace of the Lord Jesus Christ. As a friend posted on Facebook, "The Law is rigid. It demands brick, but denies me straw. But the gospel of grace is liberating. It bids me to fly and gives me wings."

FACTS ABOUT THE LAW

* **Christ is the end of the Law.** *"Christ is the end of the law for righteousness to everyone who believes"* (Romans 10:4).

* **We are delivered from the law.** *"But now we have been delivered from the law"* (Romans 7:6).

* **We are dead to the Law.** *"For I through the law died to the law that I might live to God"* (Galatians 2:19).

* **We are free from the Law.** *"For the law of the Spirit of life in Christ Jesus has made me free from the law of sin and death"* (Romans 8:2).

* **We are redeemed from the Law.** *"[Jesus came] to redeem those who were under the law"* (Galatians 4:5).

* **We are redeemed from the curse of the Law.** *"Christ has redeemed us from the curse of the law"* (Galatians 3:13).

* **We are no longer under the Law.** *"If you are led by the Spirit, you are not under the law"* (Galatians 5:18).

* **If righteousness comes by the Law, then Christ died in vain.** *"If righteousness comes through the law, then Christ died in vain"* (Galatians 2:21).

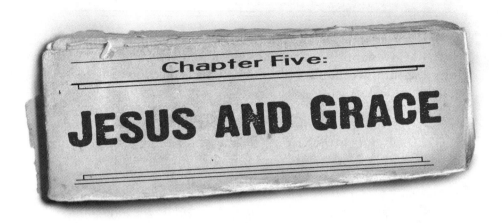

Chapter Five:

JESUS AND GRACE

Grace is all about Jesus. Everything in the Bible is about Jesus. He is more than the "Alpha" and the "Omega," He is the alpha *to* the omega. He is the "A" to the "Z" and everything in between. Joseph Prince says, "In the Old Testament, Jesus is concealed; in the New Testament, Jesus is revealed." Everything in the Old Testament points toward Jesus. Everything in the New Testament points back to Jesus. We can see Jesus in every page of the Bible. Jesus is the face of grace. The goal of studying the Bible is to see more of Jesus.

Every detail of the Old Covenant points us to what Jesus does in the New Covenant.

- The Tabernacle reveals the character of Jesus.

- The system of animal sacrifices reveals what Jesus accomplished for us on the cross.

- The Law reveals how good Jesus is and how much we need Him.

- The stories of the Old Testament teach us about the goodness of God and humanity's need of a Savior.

Let's look at some facts about Jesus and grace.

1. The coming of Jesus, the Man of grace, was prophesied under the Old Covenant. In the Old Testament, men were living under the Law. But the psalmists and the prophets spoke of a day when grace would come.

- *"...the LORD will give grace and glory; No good thing will He withhold from those who walk uprightly"* (Psalm 84:11). Notice, this verse is in the future tense. It speaks of the coming of Jesus Christ.

- *"I will pour on the house of David and on the inhabitants of Jerusalem the Spirit of grace and supplication; then they will look on Me whom they pierced"* (Zechariah 12:10).

- *"Of this salvation the prophets have inquired and searched carefully, who prophesied of the grace that would come to you"* (1 Peter 1:10).

2. Jesus came as a visible manifestation of God's grace. *"For the law was given through Moses, but grace and truth came through Jesus Christ"* (John 1:17). Notice that the Law was given, but grace came. Grace is not a thing. Grace is a Person. Jesus is God's revealed grace. Jesus is the visible expression of God's grace. If you have Jesus, you have grace. When you experience grace, you experience Jesus.

3. Grace appeared in the person of Jesus Christ. *"For the grace of God that brings salvation has appeared to all men, teaching us that, denying ungodliness and worldly lusts, we should live soberly, righteously, and godly in the present age"* (Titus 2:11-12). When Jesus appears in your life, He teaches you to live a holy life. Faith comes by hearing the Word of God. Jesus is the Word. So the more you hear about Jesus, the more faith you have in your heart and the more grace you experience. Every time you talk about Jesus and what He has done for you, you are talking about grace.

4. Jesus walked in grace from the beginning of His life. *"The Child grew and became strong in spirit, filled with wisdom; and the* *grace of God was upon Him"* (Luke 2:40).

5. Jesus was full of both grace and truth. *"And the Word became flesh and dwelt among us, and we beheld His glory, the glory as of the only begotten of the Father, full of grace and truth"* (John 1:14). Our preaching should also be full of both grace and truth. When we preach about grace, we reveal God's mercy. When we preach about truth, we reveal God's holiness and need for justice. Preaching truth without grace is harsh. Preaching grace without truth misleads people into thinking they can abuse God's grace by continuing to live a life of sin. Truth without grace becomes brutality; grace without truth becomes hypocrisy.

6. When Jesus is preached, grace is revealed. *"With great power the apostles gave witness to the resurrection of the Lord Jesus. And great grace was upon them all"* (Acts 4:33). When the apostles began sharing about the supernatural resurrection of Jesus, the early church experienced "great grace." Not "normal grace," but "great grace." The same thing happens today when we preach about the resurrection of Jesus. You might even translate this term "great grace" as "radical grace," or even "hyper-grace." It is the type of grace that Paul was talking about when he wrote, *"the grace of our Lord was exceedingly abundant"* (1 Timothy 1:14). It is overwhelming, supernatural forgiveness of sins and freedom from the old forms of religion.

7. In Jesus, we have received grace on top of grace, favor on top of favor, and blessing on top of blessing. *"And of His fullness we have all received, and grace for grace"* (John 1:16). The Amplified Version translates the last phrase of this verse as *"grace on top of grace."* This verse gives us a picture of overwhelming grace. When we give our lives to Jesus, we receive all of His fullness.

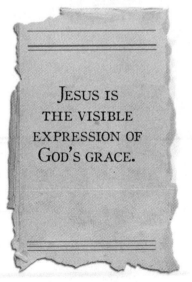

JESUS IS THE VISIBLE EXPRESSION OF GOD'S GRACE.

8. The more you know about Jesus, the less you will sin. When you meet Jesus Christ, the personification of grace, the desire to sin leaves your life. If you have given your life to Jesus and you are still bound by an addiction, the solution is not to hear how your addiction is sin. The solution is to meet Jesus in a greater way. The more you know Jesus, the less you want to sin. The grace message is not about allowing people to get away with sin. The grace message is about revealing more and more of Jesus. Are you sin-conscious or Christ-conscious? Are you thinking about what you must do, or are you thinking about what Jesus did for you?

The more you are reminded of who you are in Christ, the less you will sin. Believing in Jesus gives you an ever-greater desire to do what is right. Knowing more about Jesus does not cause you to want to sin, instead it makes you recognize that you are holy in Christ, thereby inspiring you to live in holiness.

9. God does not see your sins when they are under the blood of Jesus. Jesus is *"the Lamb of God who takes away the sin of the world!"* (John 1:29). God is not looking for a way to punish you for your sins. He is looking for a way to forgive your sins. All of God's anger and judgment was poured out on Jesus at the cross. God is not angry any longer. In the New Testament, God is revealed as a God of love.

> UNDER GRACE, IF YOU DO ONE THING RIGHT, BY MAKING JESUS THE LORD OF YOUR LIFE, YOU WILL BE MADE RIGHTEOUS IN EVERY AREA.

10. The only sin that sends people to hell is the sin of rejecting Jesus. *"When [the Holy Spirit] comes, He will convict the world of guilt in regard to sin and righteousness and judgment: in regard to sin, because men do not believe in Me"* (John 16:8-9). Over the years, many theologians have debated about "the unpardonable sin." What is this horrible sin that automatically sends people to hell? Is it murder?

No, God can forgive the murderer. Is it homosexuality? No, God is willing to forgive the homosexual. In reality, the only sin that has the power to send someone to hell is the sin of not believing in Jesus. Since it is the Holy Spirit who draws us to Jesus, the sin of blaspheming the Holy Spirit (Mark 3:29) is the sin of denying the Spirit's invitation to receive Jesus.

At the Judgment Seat, God will ask unbelievers only one question, "Did you make Jesus the Lord of your life?" We are not sinners because we sin; we are sinners because Adam sinned. We are not made righteous because we do righteous deeds; we are made righteous because Jesus is righteous. Under the Law, if you do one thing wrong, you are guilty of breaking the whole Law. Under grace, if you do one thing right, making Jesus the Lord of your life, you will be made righteous in every area. Nothing you do can earn salvation. The reverse is also true, nothing you do can cause you to lose your salvation (except the sin of turning away from trusting in Jesus for your salvation).

The only sin that can send you to hell is the sin of rejecting Jesus.

The grace of God is not some abstract concept, not some dusty word on the pages of Scripture. Amazing grace is no less than the Son of God himself, Jesus Christ. Draw near to God and He will draw near to you. Draw near to Jesus, and grace will draw near to you.

The Old Testament prophet, Isaiah, foretelling the coming of Christ, wrote this: *"'Comfort, yes, comfort My people!' says your God. Speak comfort to Jerusalem, and cry out to her, that her warfare is ended, that her iniquity is pardoned"* (Isaiah 40:1-2). Because of Christ, your warfare is ended. Because of Jesus, your iniquity is pardoned! You were an enemy of God, but by grace you have been saved, and in Christ, you are one of God's people.

When Jesus died on the cross, He paid the penalty for our sins. The cross was the most horrible torture device imagined by mankind, but God turned it into the greatest symbol of hope. Someone asked Jesus, "How much do you love me?" Jesus stretched out His hands and said, "This much." Then He died on the cross. It was not the nails that held Jesus on the cross, it was His love for you. The cross is the proof that Jesus loves you. The cross is the bridge between heaven and earth. Jesus is standing in the gap. The cross of Christ is the only answer for the Law, there is no other. The cross is the center point and the dividing line of human history. It stands between B.C. and A.D., between salvation and destruction, and between the Old Testament and the New Testament. Before the cross, mankind was separated from God; after it, we can be reconciled to God. Now I have a question for you, "Is the cross the center of your life?"

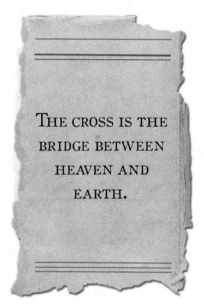

THE CROSS IS THE BRIDGE BETWEEN HEAVEN AND EARTH.

ROUND 3

Early Church Brawlers

ROUND 3

The third round of the prize fight takes place at the Jerusalem Council.

The Law is still woozy from the hit he took at the end of Round Two. Grace is looking confident, but it's unclear if she has the stamina to go the distance.

At the beginning of the round, James is in the black corner with The Law. As a good Jewish boy, he was raised to uphold The Law.

Paul is firmly in the red corner with Grace. He shouts the loudest for Grace to triumph. Peter seems unsure whose corner man he should be. He keeps walking ringside, contending earnestly with both James and Paul.

Grace strikes. The Law feints, then counterpunches. Grace strikes again with a left cross. Toe to toe, the battle is fought. Who will win? Will Grace prove stronger than The Law?

After three bruising minutes, the round is over. The judges call the round a draw. The opponents are evenly matched. The crowd watches in amazement as James walks away from the corner of The Law and joins Team Grace.

Chapter Six:
PETER & PAUL

"Repent, and let every one of you be baptized in the name of Jesus Christ for the remission of sins," Peter proclaimed on the Day of Pentecost. A crowd had gathered around him and the 120 others who had been in the upper room when the Holy Spirit visited them. Peter went on to explain: *"...and you shall receive the gift of the Holy Spirit. For the promise is to you and to your children, and to all who are afar off, as many as the Lord our God will call"* (Acts 1:38-39).

It was a powerful message! Thousands of people put their faith in Christ when they heard what Peter preached, the good news that "everyone who calls upon the name of the Lord will be saved." But it was a message that would take the preacher, Peter, a while to fully comprehend.

It was not really his fault. When legalism has chained a man's soul, it is difficult for him to allow grace to set him free. From a young age, Peter was trained to keep the Law. He knew that the Jews were God's chosen people and that he was not supposed to eat certain kinds of "unclean" animals. Peter knew the Law inside and out, and kept it as best as he could.

He was a disciple of Jesus for three years. As he followed the Master, Peter heard Him condemn the hypocrisy of the Pharisees. He watched Jesus forgive even the worst offenders of the Law. He saw Him break many of the extra laws that the Pharisees so delighted in to amplify the Law of Moses. He was himself forgiven by the risen Jesus after having betrayed Him. Peter had experienced grace in Jesus!

On the Day of Pentecost, he was filled with the Holy Spirit. He understood that sinners could be forgiven and saved by believing in Jesus Christ. He stood up and preached this good news to the thousands who were gathered in Jerusalem for the feast. Yet, Peter still needed a divine encounter in order to realize that the Law was indeed dead, and that grace was the new reality.

It was in the city of Joppa that Peter received the revelation that the Gentiles (non-Jewish people) could be saved. Joppa was the city that the Old Testament prophet Jonah had fled from when God told him to go preach salvation to the evil Gentiles who lived in Nineveh.

It was noon and Peter went up on a rooftop to pray. While he was praying, he fell into a trace and saw a vision. In his vision, he saw heaven open and a massive sheet lowered down. In the sheet were many different kinds of wild animals, insects, and birds. The sheet was full of pigs, lobsters, rabbits, and snakes. All the animals had one thing in common: they were all "unclean." This meant that according to the Law, Peter was forbidden to eat them.

A voice came from heaven, "Rise, Peter, kill and eat."

Peter recognized the voice of God, but could not believe what he was hearing. The command to eat these animals was against everything he had ever been taught. He told God, "No way am I going to eat these animals. I have never eaten anything common and unclean."

The voice said, "What God has cleansed, you must not call unclean." Peter saw this same vision three times. Then as he woke, there was a knock at the door. Three men had come from Cornelius, a Roman Centurion. Cornelius was a Gentile. He was "unclean." He was not a keeper of the Law. Under normal circumstances, Peter would have never had anything to do with such a man. But what

God had cleansed, Peter was not to call unclean. When the men asked him to go with them to the house of Cornelius, he went with them.

Peter told Cornelius and his household about Jesus and to his surprise, they were all filled with the Holy Spirit. When some of the Christians back in Jerusalem heard what had happened, they were upset with Peter for eating with a man who was uncircumcised. Peter explained to them what had happened, arguing, "If God gave them the same gift He gave us when we believed on the Lord Jesus Christ, who was I that I could withstand God?"

This silenced Peter's critics, and the believers began to rejoice that even Gentiles could receive salvation. Later Barnabas witnessed God's grace at work among the Gentiles in Antioch: *"When he came and had seen the grace of God, he was glad, and encouraged them all that with purpose of heart they should continue with the Lord"* (Acts 11:23).

Like Barnabas, we should be glad when we see grace in action. It is disappointing to hear some ministry leaders speak against the "grace message." Grace is the core of Christianity. We should always be happy when we see the grace of God at work.

Saul: Murderer of Christians

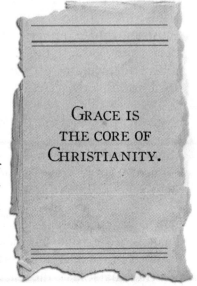

GRACE IS THE CORE OF CHRISTIANITY.

Saul was a celebrity among the Pharisees. He was circumcised on the eighth day as the Law demanded. Both of his parents were Jews of the tribe of Benjamin. He was educated in Tarsus in the philosophy of the Greeks. He studied theology in Jerusalem under the brilliant religious scholar Gamaliel, one of the leading Pharisees. He memorized the Torah. He enthusiastically kept every detail of the Law. He lived a moral lifestyle. Concerning the righteousness that is in the Law, he said he was *"blameless."* Saul was so zealous for the Law that he called himself *"a Hebrew of the Hebrews"* (Philippians 3:4-6).

Because of his passion for the Jewish faith, the followers of Christ infuriated him. "That rabble rouser Jesus was crucified," he said to himself, grinding his teeth. "Why do these people insist on saying He is alive?"

Saul developed a fearful reputation among the Christians. Everyone knew he stood by approvingly when Stephen was viciously murdered by stoning. The Council of the Pharisees gave him permission to hunt down all who belonged to the sect of the Christians. With enthusiastic energy, Saul pursued those who believed in Jesus. When he caught them, he imprisoned them, tortured them, and even killed them.

Right in the middle of his self-righteous crusade to bring justice to those who were breaking the Law, Saul had a divine encounter with grace. He was on his way to Damascus with letters from the high priest, giving Saul permission to arrest and imprison believers there, when suddenly he was knocked off his horse with a bolt of lightning. He saw a great light and heard a voice say, "Saul, Saul, why do you persecute Me?" By asking this question, Jesus condemned the very act which Saul thought would give him merit before God. In this moment, Saul saw that what he did out of his understanding of righteousness was actually an act of gross sin aimed directly at God.

Overwhelmed, Saul asked, "Who are You, Lord?"

The voice replied, "I am Jesus, whom you are persecuting." In that moment, Saul realized that Jesus was alive. The man of the Law met the Person of grace.

Due to his encounter, Saul was rendered blind. Three days later, Ananias, a Christian brother, came and prayed for him and he regained his sight. Immediately, Saul went to the synagogue and preached that Jesus is the Son of God. Later, Saul came to be known among the Gentiles as Paul. He eventually wrote two-thirds of the New Testament. His conversion from a self-righteous Pharisee into a Christian saved by grace is one of the greatest miracles in history.

Paul: First Preacher of Radical Grace

Paul became infatuated with grace. He opened most of his letters by mentioning grace and he closed his letters by praying for the recipients to receive "grace and peace." No one in the Bible has a greater understanding of grace than Paul the Apostle.

1. Grace was the core of Paul's preaching. On his first missionary trip, Paul visited Antioch of Pisidia, where he was asked to speak in the local synagogue. He stood up and preached the grace message, *"Therefore let it be known to you, brethren, that through this Man is preached to you the forgiveness of sins; and by Him everyone who believes is justified from all things from which you could not be justified by the law of Moses"* (Acts 13:38-39). Many of the Jews were upset at this message, but the Gentiles were "glad," and Paul *"persuaded them to continue in the grace of God"* (Acts 13:43).

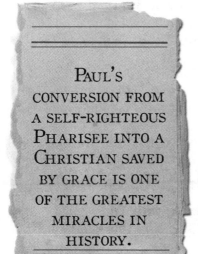

PAUL'S CONVERSION FROM A SELF-RIGHTEOUS PHARISEE INTO A CHRISTIAN SAVED BY GRACE IS ONE OF THE GREATEST MIRACLES IN HISTORY.

2. Grace enabled Paul to speak. *"For I say, through the grace given to me..."* (Romans 12:3).

3. Grace empowered Paul to write. *"I have written more boldly to you on some points...because of the grace given to me by God"* (Romans 15:15).

4. Grace is what Paul talked about at the beginning of his letters.

Paul talked about grace because

he had received grace. In the first few words of every letter he wrote, he started talking about grace.

- *"Through Him we have received grace and apostleship for obedience to the faith among all nations for His name"* (Romans 1:5).

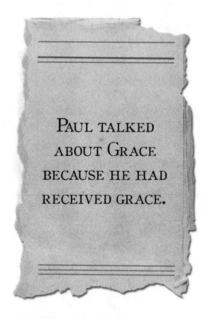

PAUL TALKED ABOUT GRACE BECAUSE HE HAD RECEIVED GRACE.

- *"Grace to you and peace from God our Father and the Lord Jesus Christ"* (1 Corinthians 1:3).

- *"Grace to you and peace from God our Father and the Lord Jesus Christ"* (2 Corinthians 1:2).

- *"Grace to you and peace from God the Father and our Lord Jesus Christ"* (Galatians 1:3).

- *"Grace to you and peace from God our Father and the Lord Jesus Christ"* (Ephesians 1:2).

- *"Grace to you and peace from God our Father and the Lord Jesus Christ"* (Philippians 1:2).

- *"To the saints and faithful brethren in Christ who are in Colosse: Grace to you and peace from God our Father and the Lord Jesus Christ"* (Colossians 1:2).

- *"To Timothy, a true son in the faith: Grace, mercy, and peace from God our Father and Jesus Christ our Lord"* (1 Timothy 1:2).

5. Grace was the subject of Paul's prayers at the end of his letters.

At the end of his letters, Paul kept returning to the theme of grace.

The greatest prayer Paul could pray was for God's grace to be given to his readers.

- "*The grace of our Lord Jesus Christ be with you. Amen*" (Romans 16:20).

- "*The grace of our Lord Jesus Christ be with you*" (1 Corinthians 16:23).

- "*The grace of the Lord Jesus Christ, and the love of God, and the communion of the Holy Spirit be with you all. Amen*" (2 Corinthians 13:14).

- "*Brethren, the grace of our Lord Jesus Christ be with your spirit. Amen*" (Galatians 6:18).

- "*Grace be with all those who love our Lord Jesus Christ in sincerity. Amen*" (Ephesians 6:24).

- "*The grace of our Lord Jesus Christ be with you all. Amen*" (Philippians 4:23).

- "*The grace of our Lord Jesus Christ be with you. Amen*" (1 Thessalonians 5:28).

- "*The grace of our Lord Jesus Christ be with you all. Amen*" (2 Thessalonians 3:18).

- "*The grace of our Lord Jesus Christ be with your spirit. Amen*" (Philemon 1:25).

5. Grace was a message Paul was willing to die for. "*But none of these things move me; nor do I count my life dear to myself, so that I may finish my race with joy, and the ministry which I received from the Lord Jesus, to testify to the gospel of the grace of God*" (Acts 20:24).

Why did Paul talk so much about grace? On a dusty road between Jerusalem and Damascus, Paul had an encounter with grace that he never forgot, an encounter that transformed his life and his destiny. Paul always wished his readers grace, because grace was the greatest gift he had ever been given. He says, *"I thank Christ Jesus our Lord who has enabled me, because He counted me faithful, putting me into the ministry, although I was formerly a blasphemer, a persecutor, and an insolent man; but I obtained mercy because I did it ignorantly in unbelief. And the grace of our Lord was exceedingly abundant, with faith and love which are in Christ Jesus. This is a faithful saying and worthy of all acceptance, that Christ Jesus came into the world to save sinners, of whom I am chief"* (1 Timothy 1:12-15).

PAUL ALWAYS WISHED HIS READERS GRACE, BECAUSE GRACE WAS THE GREATEST GIFT HE HAD EVER BEEN GIVEN.

"The chief of sinners" knew where he had come from. He knew what he deserved. But, because of God's grace, he became *"an apostle of Jesus Christ."*

Chapter Seven

THE JERUSALEM COUNCIL
Grace in Acts

The grace message is controversial today. Some preachers emphasize that we are saved by grace. Other preachers urge believers to live holy lives. Often the supporters of these two viewpoints clash. Grace preachers accuse holiness preachers of preaching the Law. Holiness preachers warn those who preach "radical grace" that their message is unbalanced and soft on sin. Others still try to combine the two views by saying that salvation comes by grace, but sanctification comes by continual effort to do what is right.

These conflicting views, along with the heated debates erupting from them, should not surprise those in the church today. After all, it is no new controversy. The roots of these arguments go all the way back to the first century church. One group within the early church was called the "Judaizers" or "The Circumcision Group" or "the sect of the Pharisees". This group taught that Gentile Christians should follow the Law of Moses. Another group led by Paul emphasized that salvation comes by faith, not by adhering in any way to the works of the Law.

The two groups and their leaders met in Jerusalem to discuss the issue. Let's peek in on their meeting and listen to what might have been said.

A former Pharisee stood up and said, "It is necessary to circumcise the Gentiles and command them to keep the Law of Moses."

Peter shared his testimony, "God gave me the vision of a sheet full of unclean animals. God told me, 'Take and eat.' At first I did not want to obey, but God repeated the instruction three times. Because of that vision, I went and ministered among the Gentiles. Many of them were saved. They were filled with the Holy Spirit, just as the Jews were. Both the Jews and the Gentiles are saved through the grace of the Lord Jesus Christ."

James, who was the chairman of the meeting, said, "Brother Paul, give us a report on what has been happening in Antioch."

Paul stood up and shared, "The Holy Spirit has moved among the Gentiles in Antioch and many have been saved through the grace of the Lord Jesus Christ. God has worked many miracles and wonders among the Gentile believers."

A Jewish believer interrupted Paul with an objection, "The problem is when Gentile believers invite Jewish believers over to their houses to partake of the Lord's Supper, the Jewish believers do not know if the food they are eating is kosher. Some Gentiles eat food that has been sacrificed to idols or even eat meat that still has blood in it."

One of the former Pharisees spoke up with anger in his voice, "The only solution is to force Gentile believers to fully keep the Law of Moses."

Paul replied calmly, "I used to be a Pharisee myself. In keeping the Law of Moses, I was blameless. But the Law did not save me. I was saved by faith in Jesus Christ, not by my pitiful attempt to keep the Law."

The Jewish believer had another comment, "But the Law must be kept—it is what makes us holy. If we tell people there is no Law, what will stop believers from lying, or stealing, or fornicating with another man's wife?"

Paul explained, "If they live according to the Spirit, they will not satisfy the lusts of the flesh. We are made holy through the grace of God. If we require Gentile converts to be circumcised and keep the Law, then we place them in the same bondage we used to be in ourselves."

The Jewish believer is horrified: "But the Gentiles eat pork—we would contaminate ourselves if we ate at their table. We would be unholy!"

Paul continued, "When Peter first came to visit Antioch, he freely ate at the table with the Gentiles. But then one of 'the Circumcision Group' came to Antioch and Peter stopped eating with the Gentile believers. This caused great confusion."

James spoke up, "I think Peter did the right thing. It would be wrong for him to flout the laws of God."

Paul spoke again, "It was hypocritical of Peter to eat with the Gentiles and then to withdraw from eating with them. Either salvation comes by works of the Law or it comes through faith in Christ. The truth is that neither the Jew nor the Greek can become righteous before God by observing the Law. So, why should we ask them to keep the Law if it cannot make them righteous?"

Peter apologized: "I never should have pulled back from fellowshipping with the Gentile believers. Sometimes it is difficult for me to understand what Paul says, but I agree with him. Salvation comes by grace. We must not put a yoke on the neck of the disciples which neither we nor our fathers were able to bear."

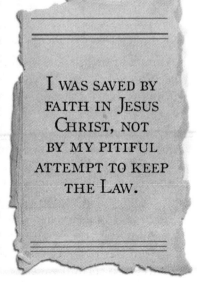

I WAS SAVED BY FAITH IN JESUS CHRIST, NOT BY MY PITIFUL ATTEMPT TO KEEP THE LAW.

Having heard all the arguments, James had the last word, "I think we should allow the Gentiles to turn to God without troubling them by forcing them to keep the Law. But, it does seem good to me that we ask them to stay away from food sacrificed to idols, and bloody meat, and sexual immorality."

All the apostles and elders in the meeting agreed with James. They wrote a letter to the believers in Antioch and asked Judas and Silas to deliver the letter. The letter said that the believers did not have to be circumcised or keep the Law of Moses. Then it continued, *"It seemed good to the Holy Spirit and to us, to lay upon you no greater burden than these necessary things..."* Then they asked them to abstain from eating food sacrificed to idols, from bloody meat, and from sexual immorality. The Gentiles were asked to abstain from these three abhorrent actions, not under the Law, but through grace. The letter ended: *"If you keep yourselves from these things, you do well"* (see Acts 15:23-29).

It Seems Good to Us

James and the Apostles were not replacing the old Law of Moses with a new law, rather they were simply making recommendations on how to live a godly life. Notice the difference between the Old Testament law that says *"Thou shalt not..."* and the New Testament recommendation, *"It seemed good to us..."* (Acts 15:28). Under Christ we have freedom, not freedom to do wrong, but freedom to choose to do what is right.

Look at what Paul tells the church in Rome, *"I beseech you therefore, brethren, by the mercies of God, that you present your bodies a living sacrifice, holy, acceptable to God, which is your reasonable service"* (Romans 12:1). Paul does not command believers to be holy, he beseeches us to be so. Paul uses the language of grace, not the language of the Law. Working for God is our "reasonable service." And we serve God, not on the basis of Law, but because of grace.

The proper role of pastors in today's society is not to enforce rules, but rather to help people live better lives. People should hear the church saying, "We love you. We care about you. We recommend the following course of action. But our recommendation comes from our desire to see God's best in you, not from a desire to force you to live a certain way."

For example, if an unmarried couple is living together, what should be the church's response? Should the church condemn them for living in sin? Or should the church recommend that the couple get married because marriage is God's best plan for the husband, wife, and children?

What should be the church's response to someone living a homosexual lifestyle? Should the homosexual be kicked out of church until he gets his life right? Should the church hit the homosexual over the head with a Bible? Or should the church lovingly recommend that being gay is not God's best way?

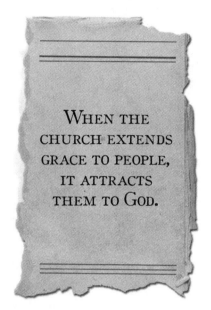

WHEN THE CHURCH EXTENDS GRACE TO PEOPLE, IT ATTRACTS THEM TO GOD.

Imagine, a couple is about to get divorced. Should the church shout, "God hates divorce—if you get divorced, you are sinning"? Or should the church explain, "It seems good to us that you work out your differences and stay together"?

When the church shouts the Law at people, it turns them away from the grace of God. But when the church extends grace to people, it attracts them to God.

Chapter Eight:

THE GRACE MANIFESTO
Grace in Romans

The book of Romans is Paul's masterpiece, his "Grace Manifesto," written to an audience composed mostly of Gentile Christians. Paul goes to great lengths to explain the fullness of the good news that is salvation in Jesus Christ. The Judaizers whom Paul debated in the Jerusalem Council had made their way to other Christian communities, including Rome, and they were trying to force these new believers to follow the laws concerning circumcision, dietary restrictions, holy days, and other things. Romans was written, in part, to combat this legalism. The central theme of Romans is that God's grace has prepared a way of salvation for people, entirely apart from the works of the Law.

Paul's argument is complicated, yet brilliant. Let's trace his line of thinking through the first ten chapters of his letter to see just what God is saying to us about His grace.

Paul begins by talking about righteousness. The righteousness that Paul speaks of is not the righteousness that comes from following a moral code; it's the righteousness that comes as we are in right relationship with God. This relationship begins by acknowledging God for who He is. (Romans 1:19-32). Because of the ungodliness of people (that is, their failure to acknowledge God for who He is) God has just cause to be angry with humans (Romans 1:18). Yet for all this justifiable anger, God is still kind, and His goodness is intent on leading people to repentance (Romans 2:4). Repentance is required of the Jew as well as the Gentile, because while the

Gentiles do not have the Law, the Jews who do have it, are guilty of breaking that same Law (Romans 2:11-24). So Gentiles who do not have the Law are unrighteous, and Jews who do have the Law cannot claim to be righteous either: *"There is no one righteous"* (Romans 3:9-20). But for both Jew and Gentile, there is a way to be right with God—Jesus Christ (Romans 3:21-22).

Paul also wants believers to have a clear understanding of the purpose and limitations of the Law. He announces this in Romans 3:20: *"Therefore by the deeds of the law no flesh shall be justified in His sight, for by the law is the knowledge of sin."* The primary limitation of the Law is that no one can become righteous by keeping it. And this is because no one has kept nor can successfully keep the Law (Christ being the only exception, Romans 3:10-12). Instead of making people righteous, the real function of the Law is to make people aware of their unrighteousness, to make people conscious of sin (Romans 3:20).

The Law ensures that everyone will be found guilty and that no one can boast that they are righteous (Romans 3:19). The problem with the Law is that it leaves everyone condemned and no one righteous. This is the trap of legalism. The observance of the Law seems to offer a way of escape from sin, but it is ultimately a blind alley, demonstrating the fruitlessness of human effort to attain righteousness this way. The dead end of the Law reveals only this: *"All have sinned and fall short of the glory of God"* (Romans 3:23). And because all have sinned, all stand in need of *"the redemption that is in Christ Jesus"* (Romans 3:24).

Paul goes on to discuss the nature of the Law and the nature of sin. While no one can be made righteous by the Law, the Law is not bad; it is not evil. In fact, it is good. The Law presents a perfect standard, holy and just (Romans 7:12). The Law is spiritual (Romans 7:14). The Law was meant to produce life (Romans 7:10). However, due to the nature of sin, the Law is woefully ineffective as a means of righteousness.

Sin has a very slippery nature. Sin exists outside of the Law, but the Law made it so that sin could be clearly defined, understood, and judged (Romans 5:13). Once the Law was in place, sin and all its ways of being lived out became definitively, unequivocally sinful, and sin became abundant (Romans 5:2, 7:7, 13). Thus the Law gave sin a whole new life: *"Apart from the law sin was dead,"* but because of the Law, *"sin revived"* and came back to life (Romans 7:8-9). Sin went on to use the Law to flex its own muscle, twisting the original intention of the Law, making it the floodgate of wrath and the legal grounds for death, rather than a means of righteousness and a source of life (Romans 4:17, 7:10). By the Law we understand not just sin, but find out that our natures are inescapably sinful, for even when we want to do what is good, we only discover that we always seem to be sinning (Romans 7:15-20). And the wages of sin is death (Romans 6:23). So we cry out in frustration: *"O wretched man that I am! Who will deliver me from this body of death?"* (Romans 7:24).

It seems a hopeless case. If the Law was the only means of being right with God, the case would indeed be hopeless. But where sin abounded, the grace of God super-abounded (Romans 5:20). So while Paul builds his argument about the Law and sin, he also outlines another means of righteousness that the super-abundant grace of God has revealed.

Paul calls Jesus the revelation and demonstration of *"the righteousness of God apart from the law"* (Romans 3:21-26). It is because of Jesus that the grace of God becomes overwhelmingly more abundant than the sin that is abundant because of the Law (Romans 5:15). Jesus fulfilled the righteous requirements of the Law—all of them (Romans 8:3). He is the only human being who has ever been, or ever will be, able to satisfy the Law of God on every point. By doing so, Jesus accomplished what the Law never could do for us: where

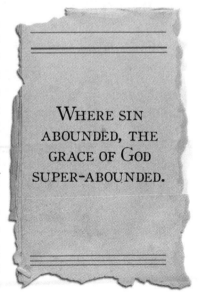

WHERE SIN ABOUNDED, THE GRACE OF GOD SUPER-ABOUNDED.

our "flesh" makes us weak and incapable of being sinless, Jesus *"condemned sin in the flesh"* (Romans 8:3). Jesus condemned sin not only by perfectly, sinlessly fulfilling the Law, but also by paying the penalty for sin under the Law, which is death. Because He did this, Jesus Christ is *"the end of the law for righteousness to everyone who believes"* (Romans 10:2-4). As the *"end of the law"* Jesus sets those who believe in Him free from sin, for *"where there is no law there is no transgression"* (Romans 4:15). So it is no longer by the works of the Law, but by faith in Jesus Christ that righteousness and right relationship with God are to be found (Romans 3:21-22, 28-30; 9:31-32). This new way of righteousness in Jesus is the essence of God's grace.

Therefore, faith, not works, is the door to righteousness. Abraham was saved, not because of any goodness of his own, any works of his own, but simply because *"[he] believed God, and it was accounted to him for righteousness"* (Romans 4:3). No one can be justified by the Law, but everyone can be made righteous by faith in Jesus (Romans 3:21-30). Romans 10:10 says that whoever believes in their heart and confesses with their mouth that Jesus Christ is Lord will be saved. Those who are saved are dead to the Law, and because they are dead to the Law, the Law no longer has any power over them (Romans 7:1-6). The new reality for the person who believes in Jesus is grace: *"For sin shall not have dominion over you, for you are not under law but under grace"* (Romans 6:14).

In Romans, the reality of grace is that there is no one and nothing left to condemn those who have put their faith in Jesus. The Law is gone. Sin has no power. God, who alone could condemn us, gave His own Son for us. Christ, who might condemn us, died for us, rose again, and lives to make intercession for us. The reality of grace is that there is now nothing that can *"separate us from the love of God which is in Christ Jesus our Lord"* (Romans 8:31-39).

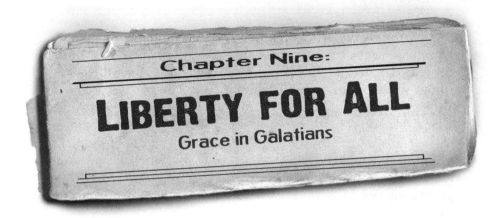

Galatians has been called the "Emancipation Proclamation for Christians." Just as Abraham Lincoln proclaimed all American slaves free, so Paul declares freedom for those who have been enslaved to the Law. Twelve times in this letter Paul uses the words "freedom" or "liberty."

Paul initially visited the region of Galatia (part of modern Turkey) during his first missionary journey. He went to the cities of Pisidia, Iconium, and Lystra in order to encourage the churches there (Acts 14:20-21). Paul's second missionary journey took him once more through the province of Galatia on the way to Mysia and Troas (Acts 16:7-8). Galatians was written either during, or just after, this second missionary journey.

In Galatians, Paul addresses people who are already believers. The Galatians were saved, but they were wondering what they had to do to be sanctified. In the book of Romans, Paul fights legalism; in Galatians, he fights a slightly different battle against what might be called "soft-legalism."

What is the difference between the two? Legalism essentially says you have to keep the Law to be saved. On the other hand, soft-legalism says you are saved by grace...but you stay saved through your good works. Some theologians have tried to separate justification and sanctification. (Traditionally, justification is the point in time when you are made righteous in God's eyes and sanctification is the process of becoming holy.) They say you are saved by faith, but that you become more sanctified over time through your actions. This is simply not true. Jesus does the work of both salvation and sanctification. If you cannot save yourself through your own efforts, how can you stay saved through your own efforts? You do not earn salvation by your works, so how could you lose it by them? According to Scripture, you are redeemed, you are righteous, and you are sanctified because of who you are in Christ Jesus: *"You are in Christ Jesus, who became for us... righteousness and sanctification and redemption"* (1 Corinthians 1:30).

Galatians was written because Paul was angry. The gospel of grace was in danger. Paul had personally led many of the Gentiles from the region of Galatia to the Lord. He taught them that salvation comes by faith in Jesus Christ. But a group of Jewish believers began teaching the churches in Galatia that Gentile believers must be circumcised and observe Jewish holidays (Galatians 4:10; 5:2; 6:12). The antagonists that Paul combats in Galatians are likely from the same group that Paul dealt with in the Jerusalem Council, the "Judaizers." Paul calls them "the circumcision party" (Galatians 2:12). The Galatian Christians who had started out by trusting Jesus for salvation were now, because of the urging of the Judaizers, turning to the works of the Law in order to "improve" their Christian walk.

After his greeting and introduction, Paul launches into a rebuke of the Galatians for forsaking his original teaching on grace: *"I marvel that you are turning away so soon from Him who called you in the grace of Christ to a different gospel"* (Galatians 1:6). He writes, *"If anyone (even an angel from heaven) preaches any other Gospel to you, let him be accursed"* (Galatians 1:8, paraphrase). If his audience didn't get the message, Paul emphatically repeats himself in the very next verse: *"If anyone preaches any other gospel to you than what you have received, let him be accursed"* (Galatians 1:9). Paul calls the Galatians *"foolish"* and *"bewitched"* (Galatians 3:1) for believing that legalism could save them or anyone. He explains that if anyone tries to keep even one part of the Law, then they must keep the whole Law (Galatians 5:3). Moreover, if someone wants to try to be justified through the Law, then Christ has no effect in that person's life and they have fallen from grace (Galatians 5:4).

In the book of Galatians, Paul defends grace with penetrating logic and Scriptural proofs. Let's look at some of his main points.

1. **You set aside the grace of God when you try to be righteous through the Law, rather than through faith in Jesus Christ (Galatians 2:21).** Other versions of this passage help us understand what Paul is saying in this verse. The Amplified version says *"I do not treat God's gracious gift as something of minor importance and defeat its very purpose."* This is what Paul is charging the Galatian believers with doing—making the sacrifice of Christ, His death on the cross, and the gift of salvation that His death paid the price for, something of little value. In fact, Paul says, Jesus' death was to no purpose if you can be right by your own work of keeping the Law.

2. **It is foolish to try to be right with God through the works of the Law.** Paul questions the Galatians: *"Are you so foolish? Having begun in the Spirit, are you now being made perfect by the flesh?"* (Galatians 3:3). Trying to improve your walk with God by the works of the Law is foolish for many reasons:

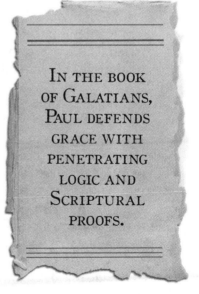

IN THE BOOK OF GALATIANS, PAUL DEFENDS GRACE WITH PENETRATING LOGIC AND SCRIPTURAL PROOFS.

• No one is justified by the Law to begin with (Galatians 2:16, 3:11). The Law was never a means of being made right with God—so it is foolishness to think that it could ever become part of that experience. Paul points out that Abraham, the father of the Jewish nation, was not made righteous through the Law. Abraham lived four hundred and thirty years before the Law was given to Moses and Israel on Sinai.

He was righteous solely because he *"believed God, and it was accounted to him for righteousness"* (Galatians 3:6).

• You actually put yourself under a curse by trying to keep the Law. *"For as many as are of the works of the law are under the curse; for it is written, 'Cursed is everyone who does not continue in all things which are written in the book of the law, to do them'"* (Galatians 3:10). If you do not obey the whole Law perfectly then you are subject to the curses that are part of disobeying the Law. What foolishness then to make the keeping of the Law part of salvation. It actually undoes the work of Christ who died on the cross to set us free from the curse of the Law (Galatians 3:13).

• Under the Law you are a slave, but under grace you are a child of God and an heir with His Son, Jesus Christ (Galatians 4:1-8). What foolishness to choose slavery over sonship, to choose bondage over freedom. But this is what the Galatians were doing, and something that believers today are often tempted to do.

3. **As those who are under grace, your identity is in Christ and is in no way any longer connected with the works of the Law.** One of the key themes of Galatians is identity. The identity of the Jews was very much wrapped up in the Law—the rite of circumcision being a significant sign of this identity. While circumcision is not an issue in the church today, the principle of what Paul says regarding circumcision is applicable to many situations in the church today.

Circumcision was at the center of the Jews' identity, and Paul uses it as a symbol of the entire system of Old Testament Law. Originally, God gave circumcision (the cutting off of the male foreskin) to Abraham and his descendants—the people of Israel—as a sign of their covenant. Circumcision set Jews apart from the Gentiles, marking them as the special people of God. But, is circumcision something that Christians have to do to be saved and included among the people of God? This was a vexing question for the early church, and one that Paul addresses.

"Indeed I, Paul, say to you that if you become circumcised, Christ will

profit you nothing" (Galatians 5:2). Paul is telling the Galatians that if they as Gentile believers submit to circumcision because of the suggestion of the Judaizers, they will have lost their faith. Instead of trusting in Christ alone for salvation, they would be relying on their own works. Paul informs them that they cannot mingle salvation by grace alone with the false righteousness that comes through works of the flesh. If the Galatians were circumcised, they would be turning their back on Christ's work on the cross.

Are we saved by faith, or are we saved by obeying the laws and fulfilling the rituals of the Old Covenant or any other traditions, however ancient or modern? Paul is not actually against circumcision or the observation of religious traditions in and of themselves. We see this in Acts 16:3 when he circumcises Timothy. In Acts 21:26, he shaves his head before visiting the Temple. It is only when someone is coerced into doing works of the flesh in order to earn salvation that Paul is against these traditions. There is nothing wrong with keeping the Sabbath, being circumcised, obeying the commandments, etc. It is only when these things are required for salvation or merit with God that they become wrong.

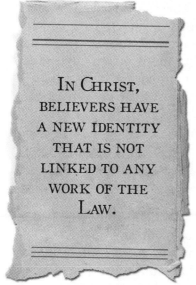

IN CHRIST, BELIEVERS HAVE A NEW IDENTITY THAT IS NOT LINKED TO ANY WORK OF THE LAW.

Some churches preach that people have to dress a certain way in order to be saved. They feel that if someone dresses "inappropriately," they are sinning and damned to hell. This kind of thinking actually teaches people to rely more on outward appearance and behavior than on faith in Christ.

In Christ, believers have a new identity that is not linked to any work of the Law: *"For in Christ Jesus neither circumcision nor uncircumcision avails anything, but a new creation"* (Galatians 6:15).

Some might argue that Abraham, the father of faith, was circumcised. However, according to Genesis 15:6 and Romans 4:3, *"Abraham believed God and it was counted unto him for righteousness."* This happened thirteen years before he was circumcised. Abraham was made righteous because of his faith, not because of circumcision. Abraham's identity is found in his faith, not in his circumcision: *"Therefore know that only those who are of faith are sons of Abraham...those who are of faith are blessed with believing Abraham"* (Galatians 3:7). It was not because Abraham was circumcised that he received the promises of God; it was because he believed God.

> TO SLIP BACK INTO THE WORKS OF THE LAW IS NO SMALL SLIP—IT IS A TUMBLE OF EPIC PROPORTIONS AND ETERNAL CONSEQUENCE.

The Judaizers did not understand the point and purpose of the Law. They thought the Law was a place of the believer's identification. But the Law was never meant to be that. Abraham's identity was not wrapped up in the Law. Israel as a nation had missed this. Their identity was wrapped up in rituals like circumcision, rather than in the faith of their founding father. The founding father of the church is Christ, the "Seed" of Abraham (Galatians 3:16), and it is through faith in Him that we are saved and live out our new identities as sons of God.

Where do you place your identity? Is your identity wrapped up in which version of the Bible you use and how many chapters of the Bible you read? In how often you go to church or what denomination you are a part of? In how much you give or serve? In whether you permit skirts to be worn above the knee or tattoos to be worn at all? What things other than faith in Christ might you be putting your trust in? Paul says this: *"You are all sons of God through faith in Christ Jesus. For as many of you as were baptized into Christ have put on Christ. There is neither Jew nor Greek, there is neither slave nor free, there is neither male nor female; for you are all one in Christ Jesus. And if you are Christ's, then you are Abraham's seed, and heirs according to the promise"* (Galatians 3:26-29).

4. **You fall from grace and become estranged from Christ when you attempt to be justified by the Law (Galatians 5:4).** When Paul talks about being *"estranged from Christ,"* he is referencing the issue of the believer's identity. How ironic! In the midst of trying to be right with God by keeping the Law, people who do so actually make themselves strangers to Him. How important it is then for believers to do as Paul says in Galatians 5:1: *"Stand fast therefore in the liberty by which Christ has made us free, and do not be entangled again with a yoke of bondage."*

To slip back into the works of the Law is no small slip—it is a tumble of epic proportions and eternal consequence. It is a fall from grace! It is giving up your wonderful identity as a child of God and an heir with Christ. It is giving up your freedom to become a slave. It is giving up all that Christ has done for the all that you can never do. Stand fast in God's grace and be free!

LAW VS GRACE

The Law is bad news for the sinner; grace is good news for the believer.

The Law reveals God's holiness; grace reveals God's love.

The Law is perfect at condemning the sinner; grace is perfect at saving the sinner.

The Law condemns; grace justifies.

The Law and grace cannot mix.

The Law keeps us from coming to God; grace invites us to come just as we are.

The Law condemns; grace forgives.

The Law punishes; grace redeems.

The Law says "Do this and live;" grace says "It is done."

The Law says "Try;" grace says "It is finished."

The law brings a curse; grace brings blessing.

The Law kills; grace saves.

The Law shuts every mouth before God; grace opens every mouth in praise of God.

The Law condemns the best of us; grace saves the worst of us.

The Law says "Pay what you owe;" grace says "The bill has been paid."

The Law says "The wages of sin is death;" grace says "The gift of God is eternal life."

The Law says "The soul that sins shall surely die;" grace says, "Believe and live."

The Law reveals our sin; grace erases our sin.

Chapter Ten:

THE GRACE OF GOOD WORKS

Grace in James

Let's look at two different Scripture passages: one is from Paul, the other from James. At first glance, these verses seem to directly contradict each other. Much of the controversy about the grace message can be resolved by a proper understanding of what each of these titans of the early church, Paul and James, really meant.

Romans 11:6 says, *"And if by grace, then it is no longer of works; otherwise grace is no longer grace. But if it is of works, it is no longer grace; otherwise work is no longer work."* Paul is saying that grace and works are mutually exclusive you are saved by grace alone without works, or it is not grace at all.

James 2:24 says the exact opposite, *"You see then that a man is justified by works, and not by faith only."* James 2:24 seems to directly contradict Romans 11:6. Paul says we are saved by grace through faith and not by works. Then James comes along and says we can be justified by our works, and not by faith alone. So, who is right?

Now compare another two verses. Paul says, *"For if Abraham was justified by works, he has something to boast about, but not before God"* (Romans 4:2). Again, James seems to say the exact opposite. *"Was not Abraham our father justified by works when he offered Isaac his son on the altar? Do you see that faith was working together with his works, and by works faith was made perfect?"* (James 2:21-22). According to James, Abraham's actions proved he had faith.

Different Revelations of God

Martin Luther was so frustrated with the book of James that he called it an "epistle of straw." He actually suggested that we throw the book of James out of the Bible. But we can't just tear pages out of the Bible if we don't like them. Instead, we must wrestle with the full counsel of God until we come to a more complete understanding of God's character.

John Calvin tried to resolve this issue by saying that when Paul uses the word "justified," he means something different from what James means when he uses the same word. For Calvin, Paul is talking about us being justified before God, but James is talking about us being justified in front of men.

Greg Fraser says, "Different people have different revelations and understanding of God. " He used the metaphor of a diamond to explain what he meant. When a diamond is held up to the light, each angle reflects a different color of light. Each facet of a diamond reveals a beautiful new view. In the same way, there are many different facets to God. He is infinite! It's impossible for the human mind to fully grasp everything there is to know about Him.

This is part of understanding both Paul and James. Paul reveals one facet of God's character; James reveals another. Paul had a revelation about grace; James had a revelation about good works. Grace and good works are both part of God's character. At first glance, the two early church leaders appear to contradict each other, but they are both looking at the same God. Both grace preachers and holiness preachers emphasize important aspects of what it means to be a Christian.

Different Contexts for Writing

In Romans, Paul was writing against legalism. He was addressing and warning believers about the dangers of looking to the Law for righteousness. But in his book, James was combating an altogether different idea—the idea that you can be saved and live like the devil. The main issue for James was not the Law, but "lawlessness." Lawlessness is the opposite of legalism. James had to address teaching in the church that said it makes no difference how someone lives because God's grace is there to save them. When we understand this important context with regard to James' teaching, it begins to clarify the seeming contradictions between him and Paul.

Paul taught that people who are under grace are free. But what about the man who thinks he understands Paul's teaching and says, "Because I am under grace, I can go to the bar and get rip-roaring drunk." Is this man acting out of grace?

Let's look at what James said: *"But be doers of the word, and not hearers only, deceiving yourselves. For if anyone is a hearer of the word and not a doer, he is like a man observing his natural face in a mirror; for he observes himself, goes away, and immediately forgets what kind of man he was. But he who looks into the perfect law of liberty and continues in it, and is not a forgetful hearer but a doer of the work, this one will be blessed in what he does"* (James 1:22-25).

Incidentally, Paul affirms this same idea when he writes, *"For not the hearers of the law are just in the sight of God, but the doers of the law will be justified"* (Romans 2:13).

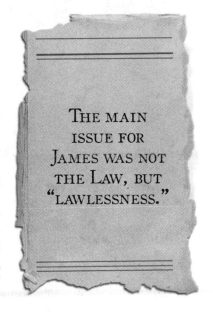

Also, John emphasizes the importance of "doing" (keeping) God's commandments when he writes, *"Blessed are those who do His commandments, that they may have the right to the tree of life, and may enter through the gates into the city. But outside are dogs and sorcerers and sexually immoral and murderers and idolaters, and whoever loves and practices a lie"* (Revelation 22:14-15). Notice

THE MAIN ISSUE FOR JAMES WAS NOT THE LAW, BUT "LAWLESSNESS."

that in this verse, the first, second, sixth, seventh, and ninth commandments are referred to.

Grace, Faith, and Good Works

"Thus also faith by itself, if it does not have works, is dead" (James 2:17). In this passage, the word "works" means corresponding actions. In other words, your actions correspond (line up) with what you believe. If you have faith, then you will have corresponding action. But action without corresponding faith is just as dead. According to James, you must believe right…and live right.

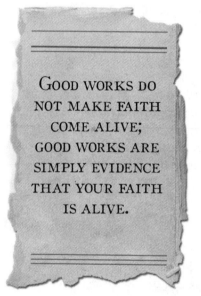

GOOD WORKS DO NOT MAKE FAITH COME ALIVE; GOOD WORKS ARE SIMPLY EVIDENCE THAT YOUR FAITH IS ALIVE.

Good works do not make faith come alive; good works are simply evidence that your faith is alive. You are not saved by faith and works; you are saved by faith that works. True faith will always have corresponding action. If you really believe, you will have corresponding actions in your life. If there is no corresponding action, there is no faith either. The grace in our lives is proven by the "good works" we do. The Reformers said, "It is faith, alone, which saves, but the faith that saves is not alone."

Works prove you have faith. If you have faith, then you will exhibit the fruit of faith. *"But someone will say, 'You have faith, and I have works.' Show me your faith without your works, and I will show you my faith by my works"* (James 2:18). Our actions should line up with what we believe. One good example of this is the sacrament of baptism. Being dunked in water does not have any power to save you by itself, otherwise every child at the public swimming pool would be saved. However, baptism is important because it is an outward sign of an inward conversion. The deed of baptism does not save you, but it is a sign (evidence) that you are saved.

Works makes our faith perfect. *"Do you see that faith was working together with his works, and by works faith was made perfect? And the Scripture was fulfilled which says, Abraham believed God, and it was accounted to him for righteousness. And he was called the friend of God. You see then that a man is justified by works, and not by faith only"* (James 2:22-24). Faith is not perfect without works. Believing is a verb, not a noun. You have to do something to show that you have faith. Faith can only be seen when it is demonstrated. Faith is invisible. Our works are like the "skin" put on our faith to show its existence and form.

Good works are a fruit of grace, not the root of grace. So if we don't do good works to get saved or to stay saved, why do we do good works? If good works do not help us earn salvation, what role do they play in the Christian faith?

On the track to heaven, there is a train. The black locomotive at the front of the train is spewing smoke and chugging away. Following it are many boxcars of different shapes and sizes. At the back of the train is a caboose, bright red and shiny.

On the side of the locomotive, painted in giant letters, is the word "GRACE." Directly behind the locomotive, the first boxcar is labeled "Righteousness." The other boxcars all contain the blessings of God. One is "healing," another is "prosperity," a third is "wisdom." And there are many more cars leading us down to the last car—the red caboose at the end of the train. The label on it reads "good works."

So, the grace locomotive is pulling the entire train toward heaven. But religious people get so impressed by the shiny red caboose that they put it right at the front of the train, trying to get good works to pull all the weight. The problem is that the caboose lacks an engine. Good works makes a great follower, but it has no power to pull the train. Good works follow salvation, but they cannot produce salvation or any of the other blessings of God. Unfortunately some religious people put the caboose at the front of the train, and the "good works" train stays stuck in the station. One preacher noted, "Good works are the fruit of salvation, not the root of salvation." Works don't save you, but they are your response to being saved.

Good works are the fruit of a Christian life. What kind of fruit is your life producing? If the tree is good, it will bear good fruit. If the tree is bad, the tree will bear bad fruit. *"Even so, every good tree bears good fruit, but a bad tree bears bad fruit. A good tree cannot bear bad fruit, nor can a bad tree bear good fruit. Every tree that does not bear good fruit is cut down and thrown into the fire. Therefore by their fruits you will know them"* (Matthew 7:17-20). If you are living the life of faith, you will produce the fruit of faith, and good works are part of that fruit.

What if you don't have any good works? *"And seeing a fig tree by the road, He came to it and found nothing on it but leaves, and said to it, 'Let no fruit grow on you ever again.' Immediately the fig tree withered away"* (Matthew 21:19). Jesus came to a fig tree and found that while it had lots of leaves, it wasn't bearing any fruit, and had nothing to offer Him. Good works are part of the fruit that we can offer to God and to others for His sake. If you do not bear good fruit, what use are you to the Kingdom of God? John 15:1-2 says this about those who don't bear any fruit: *"I am the true vine, and My Father is the vinedresser. Every branch in Me that does not bear fruit He takes away; and every branch that bears fruit He prunes, that it may bear more fruit."*

Grace empowers you for good works. The same faith that got you saved is the faith that will help you do what is right. When you read a commandment from God in the Bible, you don't have to suffer from a sinking feeling that you will never be able to obey the instruction. Instead you can live with the knowledge that through grace, all things are possible.

The beginning of grace is eternal life and forgiveness of sin, but grace is so much more. God's grace extends to every area of your life. Bad habits, negative thought processes, and addictions can all be changed through grace.

There is grace available to help you with your actions, in the same way that there is grace to help you with your believing. Joseph Prince says, "Right living is the result of right believing." Once you believe you are saved through grace, then your actions will start to line up with your belief.

Even Paul labored and strived: *"To this end I also labor, striving according to His working which works in me mightily"* (Colossians 1:29). But notice, he labored *"according to His [Jesus'] working."* *"But by the grace of God I am what I am, and His grace toward me was not in vain; but I labored more abundantly than they all, yet not I, but the grace of God which was with me"* (1 Corinthians 15:10). The grace of God is power to let good work be done in and through you.

Grace Changes the Motivation for Doing Good Works.

I am not married because I help my wife, Jessica, in the kitchen; I help my wife in the kitchen because I am married. When I help Jessica with housework, my work does not make me more married. I simply help her because I'm her husband. In the same way, you cannot become more righteous through what you do for God, but rather you are excited to serve God because you are righteous.

Under the New Covenant, our motives become more important than our actions. It's all about motivation. You can have the exact same action with the wrong motivation. A woman forced to have sex is raped. A woman paid to have sex is a prostitute. A woman who willing gives her body to the man she is married to is a wife. In all three cases, the outward action is the same (sex has occurred), but the motivation determines whether the act is a loving action or a repulsive one.

God's grace is a believer's motivation for good works, but "religion" is a whore. Our relationship with Jesus should be like a marriage. Jesus is the bridegroom and the Church is the bride. The marriage bed is all about relationship. But religion is like a man who visits a prostitute. The physical action might be the same, but the love and covenant is absent.

Once there were two restaurant owners. The owner of The Grace Café was an immigrant who was proud of living in his new country. He put a huge American flag on a pole right in front of his restaurant. Because of his patriotism, people flocked to eat his food. When the restaurant owner across the street saw the increased traffic because of the flag, he put up his own flag, not because he was patriotic, but because he wanted more business. Both restaurants now have identical flags, but there is a difference in their motives. The first owner has a "flag with patriotism," the second owner has a "flag without patriotism."

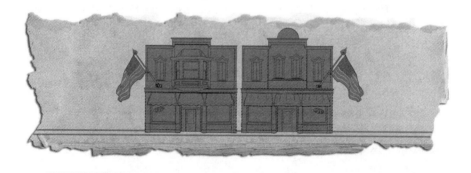

In the same way, some people do good works because of grace and others do good works in an effort to get grace or look like they have grace. One Christian man tithes because he is in bondage to legalism. He has been taught from the Old Testament that he will be under a curse if he fails to tithe. Another Christian man tithes because he loves God and gives ten percent out of a motive of gratitude. They both put the same amount of money into the same offering plate, but one does it out of legalism and the other does it out of love. One is the equivalent of a spiritual prostitute, while the other is part of the bride of Christ.

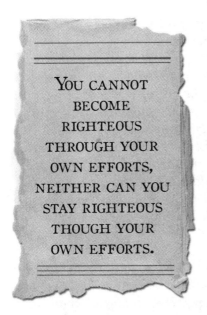

YOU CANNOT BECOME RIGHTEOUS THROUGH YOUR OWN EFFORTS, NEITHER CAN YOU STAY RIGHTEOUS THOUGH YOUR OWN EFFORTS.

One man refuses to drink alcohol because he thinks it is a terrible sin. Another man refuses to drink alcohol because he has a revelation that his body is the temple of the Holy Spirit, and he does not want to pollute that temple. Same behavior—not drinking alcohol—but one man is motivated by legalism; the other is motivated by grace.

You cannot become righteous through your own efforts; neither can you stay righteous though your own efforts. You need God's help to change ingrained sinful habits. For many, the desire to change becomes a daily struggle with the flesh. This leads to a "works mentality," where people try to do what is right. But even if they manage to keep their outward actions right, many still fight with inward temptation.

Doing the right thing is of little value when one inwardly wants to sin. The only truth that can set us free, both inwardly and outwardly, is God's grace. Jesus said, *"Come to Me, all you who labor and are heavy laden, and I will give you rest"* (Matthew

11:28). For us to truly be free of the heavy burden of temptation—temptation to sin and temptation to trust in our own attempts at good behavior—we must come to Jesus, the personification of grace. Our self-effort is worthless. We must learn to rely on Jesus. Through Jesus, victory over sin becomes easy.

Good Works Display God's Grace to Our World.

For a world that needs to experience God's grace, our good works are important.

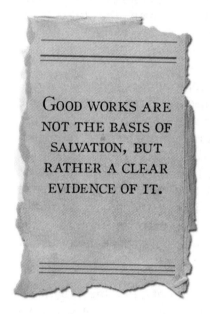

GOOD WORKS ARE NOT THE BASIS OF SALVATION, BUT RATHER A CLEAR EVIDENCE OF IT.

Good works are part of God's eternal plan for your life: *"For by grace you have been saved through faith, and that not of yourselves; it is the gift of God, not of works, lest anyone should boast. For we are His workmanship, created in Christ Jesus for good works, which God prepared beforehand that we should walk in them"* (Ephesians 2:8-10). We are not saved by good works, but we were created to do them!

Paul wrote to Titus, *"This is a faithful saying, and these things I want you to affirm constantly, that those who have believed in God should be careful to maintain good works. These things are good and profitable to men"* (Titus 3:8).

Jesus equated good works with the believer's role of being light in a dark world: *"Let your light so shine before men, that they may see your good works and glorify your Father in heaven"* (Matthew 5:16). Our Father is a good God, and He is revealed in the light of the good works done by His children.

For this reason, we are to be zealous for good works: *"For the grace of God that brings salvation has appeared to all men, teaching us that, denying ungodliness and worldly lusts, we should live soberly, righteously, and godly in the present age, looking for the blessed hope and glorious appearing of our great God and Savior Jesus Christ, who gave Himself for us, that He might redeem us from every lawless deed and purify for Himself His own special people, zealous for good works"* (Titus 2:11-14).

Paul and James had different revelations of God, therefore, they appear to disagree about the place of good works in the life of those who belong to Christ. However, they did agree that good works are not the basis of salvation, but rather a clear evidence of it. James would have no problem with Paul's final prayer for the Thessalonians:

"Now may our Lord Jesus Christ Himself, and our God and Father, who has loved us and given us everlasting consolation and good hope by grace, comfort your hearts and establish you in every good word and work" (2 Thessalonians 2:16-17).

LAW VS GRACE

The Law was written on stone; grace is written on our hearts.

The Law brings bondage; grace gives liberty.

The Law is powered by fear; grace brings peace.

The Law depends on man's ability; grace relies upon God's ability.

The Law is a ministry of death; grace is a ministry of life.

The Law demands righteousness; grace imparts righteousness.

The Law commands us to be perfect; grace makes us perfect.

The Law gives us a religion; grace gives us a relationship with God.

The Law is bad news for the sinner; grace is good news for the believer.

The Law condemns the sinner; grace justifies the believer.

The Law is all about God's need for justice; grace is all about God's love for mercy.

"The law tells me how crooked I am; grace comes along and straightens me out." - D. L. Moody

"The law can only chase a man to Calvary, no further." - D.L. Moody

"The law reveals the sickness; grace provides the cure." - Daniel Kerr

"The law orders; grace supplies the power of acting." – Augustine

My wife Jessica noticed that my tee-shirts were starting to look ratty because of holes and stains, so she went to the store and bought me some new ones. When she returned home, she threw all of my old shirts into the rag pile. She threw out the old to make room for the new.

The same thing happened when the New Covenant came along. Hebrews explains that the New Covenant makes the Old Covenant obsolete. In Galatians and Romans, Paul mostly writes to Gentile believers. But the author of Hebrews writes primarily to Jewish believers and explains the concept of grace in Jewish terms. By talking about the tabernacle, the priesthood, the system of offering sacrifices, and the great heroes of the Jewish faith, he demonstrates how Jesus completely fulfilled every aspect of Jewish tradition. Let's look at some facts about the New Covenant from the book of Hebrews.

1. Christ is the guarantee of the New Covenant. *"Jesus has become a surety of a better covenant"* (Hebrews 7:22, 8:6).

2. The New Covenant replaces the Old Covenant. *"For if that first covenant had been faultless, then no place would have been sought for a second. Because finding fault with them, He says: 'Behold, the days are coming, says the Lord, when I will make a new covenant with the house of Israel'* (Hebrews 8:7-8).

3. The Old Covenant is more than replaced; it is gone. *"In that He says, 'A new covenant,' He has made the first obsolete. Now what is becoming obsolete and growing old is ready to vanish away"* (Hebrews 8:13).

4. The New Covenant is much better than the Old Covenant. In Exodus 20, the Ten Commandments say, *"You shall not....you shall not...you shall not."* But in Hebrews 8:8-12, God says, *"I will...I will...I will."* In the Old Covenant, the emphasis is on what we have to do, but in the New Covenant, the emphasis is on what God does for us. We are now *"ministers of the new covenant"* (2 Corinthians 3:6).

5. Under the Old Covenant, the Law never made you perfect. *"For the law made nothing perfect; on the other hand, there is the bringing in of a better hope, through which we draw near to God"* (Hebrews 7:19).

6. Under the New Covenant, Jesus is our perfect High Priest who stands before God on our behalf. *"For such a High Priest was fitting for us, who is holy, harmless, undefiled, separate from sinners, and has become higher than the heavens; who does not need daily, as those high priests, to offer up sacrifices, first for His own sins and then for the people's, for this He did once for all when He offered up Himself"* (Hebrews 7:26-27).

7. Under the Old Covenant, we had inferior high priests, but under the New Covenant, our High Priest is perfect. *"For the law appoints as high priests men who have weakness, but the word of the oath, which came after the law, appoints the Son who has been perfected forever"* (Hebrews 7:28).

8. Under the New Covenant, God's law is written on our hearts. *"For this is the covenant that I will make with the house of Israel after those days, says the LORD: I will put My laws in their mind and write them on their hearts; and I will be their God, and they shall be My people"* (Hebrews 8:10). God is not about a list of rules, He is after relationship.

9. Under the New Covenant, God no longer remembers your sin. *"For I will be merciful to their unrighteousness, and their sins and their lawless deeds I will remember no more"* (Hebrews 8:12). In Christ, your sin is completely gone. Not only do you have a new future, you also have a new past. All our sins--past, present, and future--were taken away at the cross of Jesus.

We remember our sins and the sins of others better than God remembers them. If we ask God, "What about Bob who committed adultery?" God replies, "I don't remember him committing adultery." God chooses not to remember the sins that are covered by the blood of Jesus. Scripture repeatedly affirms this:

- *"As far as the east is from the west, so far has He removed our transgressions from us"* (Psalm 103:12).

- *"I have blotted out, like a thick cloud, your transgressions, And like a cloud, your sins. Return to Me, for I have redeemed you"* (Isaiah 44:22).

- *"For I will forgive their iniquity, and their sin I will remember no more"* (Jeremiah 31:34).

- *"He will again have compassion on us, And will subdue our iniquities. You will cast all our sins into the depths of the sea"* (Micah 7:19).

- *"By that will [the will of God] we have been sanctified through the offering of the body of Jesus Christ once for all"* (Hebrews 10:10).

- *"Their sins and their lawless deeds I will remember no more"* (Hebrews 10:17).

WE REMEMBER OUR SINS AND THE SINS OF OTHERS BETTER THAN GOD REMEMBERS THEM.

Some say that when you become a Christian, all your past sins are forgiven. But they go on to say that each time you sin while you are a Christian, you must go back to Jesus and ask forgiveness again and again and again. And heaven forbid that you should die without one of these sins confessed and forgiveness asked for!

When Jesus died, how many of your sins were still in the future? The answer is "all of them." The work He did on the cross covers all your sins: past, present, and future.

Getting Saved Repeatedly

When I was six years old, my parents took me to children's church. The children's pastor gave us an opportunity to ask Jesus to forgive our sins. My heart was tender toward God, so I went to the altar and prayed the sinner's prayer. Several days later, I lied to my mother and felt bad about it. So the next Sunday, I went to the altar to get saved again. In fact, every week I did something wrong, so I felt like I had to get saved again every Sunday.

After several weeks, the children's pastor pulled me aside. He said, "Daniel, why do you come up front to get saved every week?"

"Because I did something wrong," I explained, "I need forgiveness."

The children's pastor explained to me, "You don't need to get saved again every week. Once you get saved, Jesus forgives all your sin."

God lives outside of time. When God forgave your sins, He saw everything you have ever done in your life and placed it all under the blood of Jesus. Jesus has *"forgiven you all trespasses"* (Colossians 2:13). Jesus *"bore our sins"* (1 Peter 2:24), *"gave Himself for our sins"* (Galatians 1:3), and *"purged our sins"* (Hebrews 1:3).

When you sin, God still looks at you through grace-tinted glasses. All your sins were placed on Jesus at the cross. *"For by one offering He hath perfected forever them that are sanctified"* (Hebrews 10:14 KJV). Through the shed blood of Jesus, you are made forever perfect. All your sins are gone. Jesus was punished on your behalf.

"In Him we have redemption through His blood, the forgiveness of sins, according to the riches of His grace" (Ephesians 1:7).

What About 1 John 1:9?

In light of these previous verses, let us look at one of the most controversial issues in the message of "radical grace." First John 1:9 says, *"If we confess our sins, He is faithful and just to forgive us our sins and to cleanse us from all unrighteousness."* First, I want you to know that I believe in this verse and I preach this verse. Every sinner needs to confess his or her sins to God. When we confess our sins, we are forgiven and cleansed. It is important to confess our sins to God.

The word "confess" in 1 John 1:9, in the Greek language, is a present subjunctive, first person plural. The fact that it is first person plural shows that John is including himself in this statement. Thus, this verse is addressed to both believers and unbelievers.

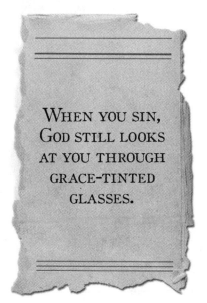

WHEN YOU SIN, GOD STILL LOOKS AT YOU THROUGH GRACE-TINTED GLASSES.

The fact that it is present implies continuous confession, therefore this confession of sins can happen more than once.

Jesus taught us to pray in the Lord's Prayer, *"Forgive us our debts, as we forgive our debtors"* (Matthew 6:12). Jesus taught His disciples to ask for forgiveness.

In Revelation 3:3, Jesus tells the church in Sardis to "repent." Apparently, Jesus felt that even though the church in Sardis was full of born-again believers, some of them still needed to repent. In Acts 8:22, Peter tells Simon the Sorcerer to repent, even after Simon believes and is baptized.

In my marriage, it never hurts to say "I'm sorry" to my wife when I have done something to hurt her.

As a believer, you do not confess in order to maintain your salvation, rather you confess to restore fellowship with God in much the same way that a child says "I'm sorry" to his father after being disobedient. My son Caleb never stops being my son no matter what he does, but when he does something wrong, it is good for him to apologize.

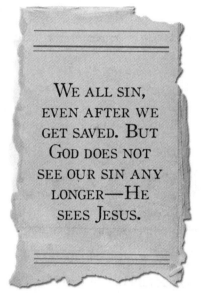

WE ALL SIN, EVEN AFTER WE GET SAVED. BUT GOD DOES NOT SEE OUR SIN ANY LONGER—HE SEES JESUS.

Furthermore, John brackets 1 John 1:9 with two other important points. He writes, *"If we say that we have no sin, we deceive ourselves, and the truth is not in us"* (1 John 1:8), and *"If we say that we have not sinned, we make Him a liar, and His word is not in us"* (1 John 1:10).

We all sin, even after we get saved. But God does not see our sin any longer—He sees Jesus. This is why John writes, *"My little children, these things I write to you, so that you may not sin. And if anyone sins, we have an Advocate with the Father, Jesus Christ the righteous. And He Himself is the propitiation for our sins, and not for ours only but also for the whole world"* (1 John 2:1-2). If we do sin, we have an Advocate who stands between God and us.

In Jesus, there is no sin. When God looks at someone who has been born again, He sees Jesus standing there in our place. *"You know that He was manifested to take away our sins, and in Him there is no sin"* (1 John 3:5).

So, 1 John 1:9 must be read in light of these verses:

- *"Whoever abides in Him does not sin"* (1 John 3:6).

- *"He who sins is of the devil"* (1 John 3:8).

- *"Whoever has been born of God does not sin [and] cannot sin"* (1 John 3:9).

Some translations change these verses to say, "Whoever has been born of God does not [continue] to sin." This is used to teach that the sin these verses are talking about is a continuous, habitual sin. However, this translation is not supported by the Greek tense used in these verses. The word "cannot" in 1 John 3:9 is the Greek word *ou dunatai* which can be translated as "not able" or "not have the power" to sin.

According to the plain reading of 1 John 3:9, if you abide in Jesus, you do not sin. If you have been born of God, you do not sin and you cannot sin. If you do not sin, then in God's eyes you do not need to confess your sins all the time.

Today, some people in the church feel that if they miss confessing a single sin, their salvation is in jeopardy. So, what happens if they forget to confess a sin? What if Jesus comes back in the twinkling of an eye and they have not had a chance to confess yet? I do not base my eternal security on whether I have confessed every sin or not. If I did, I would always worry that I had missed one. However, I think it is right for us to humble ourselves before God and say, "Sorry for messing up."

There is a "grace way" to confess your sins, and there is a legalistic way to confess your sins. In the Roman Catholic Church, people confess their sins to a priest. Before Martin Luther had a revelation about grace, he was so concerned about confessing every sin that once he sat with a priest for over six hours in order to confess every single thing he had done wrong. He confessed every sin of commission and every sin of omission. He carefully searched his memory for every sin he had ever committed. At that time, he believed that "Sins to be forgiven must be confessed. To be confessed they must be recognized and remembered. If they are not recognized and remembered, they cannot be confessed. If they are not confessed, they are not forgiven." Yet, despite all this effort, he still felt sinful in front of a righteous Judge. Finally, the priest got tired and said, "Martin, just go home."

The legalistic confessor says, "Forgive me for lusting after that woman.

Forgive me for doubting you for a second. Forgive me for telling a white lie. Forgive me for my lack of faith. Forgive me for that angry thought." Once you start listing all your sins, you will never run out of things to repent of.

In contrast, the person who understands grace says to God, "Thank You for forgiving me. Thank You that I am the righteousness of God in Christ Jesus. Thank You that the blood of Jesus covers all of my sins. Thank You for giving me the grace to overcome every sin." This is how we *"hold fast the confession of our hope without wavering, for He who promised is faithful"* (Hebrews 10:23). The sinner confesses his sins, the believer confesses his hope in Christ.

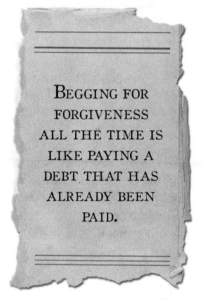

BEGGING FOR FORGIVENESS ALL THE TIME IS LIKE PAYING A DEBT THAT HAS ALREADY BEEN PAID.

The word "confess" comes from the Greek word *homologos* which is a compound word from "homo" meaning "same" and "logos" meaning "word." So, the word "confess" means to say the same words Jesus is saying. When we confess our sins, it means we say the same word about our sins that Jesus is saying. What is Jesus saying? He is saying, *"Son, your sins are forgiven you"* (Matthew 9:2). You are already forgiven, so if you make a mistake, just tell God you are sorry and say, "Thank You, Jesus, my sins are forgiven."

When God looks at you, all He sees is the righteousness of Christ Jesus. Begging for forgiveness all the time is like paying a debt that has already been paid. Imagine if someone completely paid off your mortgage. If you continued to write checks to the mortgage company every month, you would be foolish.

Under the New Covenant, your debt has been completely paid off. Stop trying to pay it again through your prayers, your confessions, or your good works.

Chapter Twelve: THE TWO MOUNTAINS

Many mountains find their way into the pages of Scripture, but two mountains stand out. Mount Sinai, where the Ten Commandments and the whole Law were given to Moses, dominates the Old Testament. Calvary, the peak on which Jesus was crucified, dominates the New Testament. Which mountain are you living on?

Mount Sinai

Mount Sinai is a symbol of the Law. With an amazing series of miracles, God brought the children of Israel out of Egypt. God put the wealth of their slave masters into their hands. He parted the Red Sea and destroyed the Egyptian army that was pursuing them. God brought the children of Israel out of Egypt, not because of their obedience, but because of His grace.

Almost immediately, the children of Israel started to complain. So, God gives them the Ten Commandments to show the seriousness of their sins. First, He reminds them of His goodness, *"You have seen what I did to the Egyptians, and how I bore you on eagles' wings and brought you to Myself"* (Exodus 19:4). He points out that He delivered them from Egypt through His grace, but then He adds conditions to future blessings by saying, *"Now therefore, if you will indeed obey My voice and keep My covenant, then you shall be a special treasure to Me above all people"* (Exodus 19:5). When they first came out of Egypt, God blessed them out of His love, but now God puts them under "conditional blessing." He says "If you obey me, then I will bless you."

The children of Israel were confident they could do anything God asked of them. *"All the people answered together and said, 'All that the LORD has spoken we will do'"* (Exodus 19:8). They boldly promised, "We will do everything You tell us to do." They chose to live under God's conditional blessing,the Law, rather than God's grace.

They thought they could "do" enough to keep God happy. But in order to show them their utter helplessness, He gave them a perfect revelation of the requirements for earning a place in heaven. God met with the Israelites at Mount Sinai. With thunder, lightning, the sound of trumpets, and billowing smoke, God spoke to them in a deep roaring voice. With bowed heads and trembling knees, the people listened as God gave them the Ten Commandments:

1. You shall have no other gods before Me.

2. You shall not bow before a carved image.

3. You shall not take the name of the Lord your God in vain.

4. You shall remember the Sabbath day, to keep it holy.

5. You shall honor your father and mother.

6. You shall not murder.

7. You shall not commit adultery.

8. You shall not steal.

9. You shall not bear false witness against your neighbor.

10. You shall not covet from your neighbor.

The people of Israel were not comforted by this experience of God, rather they were terrified. They begged Moses, "You listen to God and tell us what He says. If we hear His voice anymore, we will die."

For forty days, God met with Moses on top of Mount Sinai. While they spoke together, God gave Moses instructions to guide the Israelites in their daily lives. From His wisdom, God gave them dietary laws, ceremonial laws, ethical laws, and most important of all, God wrote the Ten Commandments with His finger on two stone tablets.

In giving the Law, God knew that the children of Israel would fail in keeping His requirements. There was no way any human being could obey all the laws God had given Moses. The Law was too perfect. It was simply impossible to keep. But God gave the Law because He wanted the Israelites to realize their need for a Savior. Once they realized how impossible it was to obey the Law, the people would appreciate God's grace all the more.

As Moses came down from the mountain, he saw that in his absence his brother Aaron had led the Israelites into sin by building a golden calf, a direct violation of the first two commandments. In anger, Moses threw the tablets of stone to the ground, shattering them into a thousand pieces. (Thus, Moses became the first man to break all Ten Commandments at the same time.)

Over the centuries, the Law worked just as God knew it would. The Israelites struggled to keep the Law, yet over and over again, they continued to break it. For forty years, they wandered in the wilderness because they broke the Law. Once they finally entered the Promised Land, they went through cycles where the children of Israel did evil in the sight of the Lord." They were punished for their evil, but then a judge would deliver them. Then for a short time they would live in peace, prosperity, and blessing. But, inevitably, the people would fall away from God once again. Later, they demanded a king, but the kings of Judah and Israel

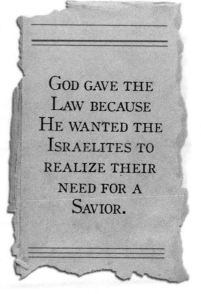

GOD GAVE THE LAW BECAUSE HE WANTED THE ISRAELITES TO REALIZE THEIR NEED FOR A SAVIOR.

fared no better at keeping the nation on the straight and narrow. One king would follow the Lord, keeping the Law to an extent, and experience blessing for himself and the kingdom. But the next king would do evil in the sight of the Lord and everyone would suffer for it.

One writer in Proverbs noted *"your law is truth"* and the psalmists sang, *"I love your law!"* But despite this devotion, no one was able to keep the Law. When the Old Testament writers say how good the Law is, they were still waiting for salvation.

The Prophetic books are full of lamentations and condemnations because Israel prostituted herself and wandered away from God. In punishment, the people of God are led away into captivity. Once they returned from captivity, the Jews became serious about keeping the Law. Rabbis arose who debated every small detail of the Law of Moses. To be on the safe side, they intensified the Law. If God said to keep the Sabbath, the rabbis taught, no cooking on the Sabbath, no riding a donkey on the Sabbath, and no lighting a match on the Sabbath. They forgot the purpose of the Sabbath— they made it a day of hassle instead of a day of rest. But for all their work, it was the same old story in the end. No matter how hard these "teachers of the Law" tried to keep the Law, they failed. They became hypocrites, keeping the Law on the outside, but failing to obey the inward dictates of the Law. They imposed horrible burdens on others that they themselves were unable to keep.

Usually, when we read the Old Testament, we focus on the stories of victory. David defeats Goliath. Solomon builds the temple. Esther rescues her people. But taken as a whole, the Old Testament is the sad story of a huge failure. It is a story of a people who could not keep God's Law. Despite centuries of striving to obey the Law, the utter failure to keep the Law given on Mount Sinai reveals the need for a Savior.

Calvary

I can hear the words of the old hymn:

On a hill far away, stood an old rugged cross,
The emblem of suffering and shame;
And I love that old cross where the dearest and best
For a world of lost sinners was slain.

Picture the mount of Calvary with three crosses standing there, and in the middle was the one where Jesus was crucified! No lightning. No thunder. No sound of trumpet blasting. No smoke. No Law being pronounced. No terror for me. Only Jesus saying, "Father, forgive them!"

Under the Law of Moses, sacrificing an animal could temporarily cover sin. For thousands of years, God's people sacrificed cows, sheep, and goats in an effort to cover their sins. Symbolically, innocent lambs bore the punishment when a person broke the Law. If the person sinned again, another lamb had to be sacrificed. But on Calvary, Jesus became the ultimate sacrificial Lamb. At the cross, Jesus took upon His body the punishment for every law that had ever been broken. All of God's need for justice was poured out upon Jesus. All of God's judgment, wrath, and anger was placed on Jesus. Even though He had never sinned, Jesus was punished for the sins of the entire world. As Jesus died, He cried out, "It is finished!" Jesus did all that needed to be done to save sinners—there was nothing left for them to do.

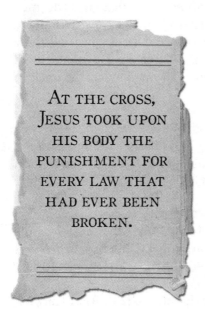

AT THE CROSS, JESUS TOOK UPON HIS BODY THE PUNISHMENT FOR EVERY LAW THAT HAD EVER BEEN BROKEN.

At the moment of Jesus' death, a veil in the temple—a massive curtain, woven three inches thick that divided the Holy of Holies from the Holy Place—was torn from top to bottom. Because of Calvary, there is no longer a separation between God and man. In the past, no one could enter the Holy of Holies, but after Jesus died on the cross, it became accessible to everyone.

Jesus provided a new way for us to become righteous. *"By Him everyone who believes is justified from all things from which you could not be justified by the law of Moses"* (Acts 13:38-39). When Jesus died a painful death on Calvary, He made it possible for us to be justified. This is something the Law of Moses was never able to accomplish. One moment at Calvary will set you free from wandering around Mount Sinai.

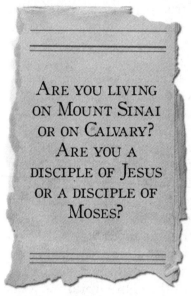

ARE YOU LIVING ON MOUNT SINAI OR ON CALVARY? ARE YOU A DISCIPLE OF JESUS OR A DISCIPLE OF MOSES?

In the Old Testament, no blemished, crippled, or defective animal or man could enter the temple. But in the New Testament, Jesus invited the poor, the crippled, the lame, and the blind. Grace made room for the imperfect.

In the Old Testament, the Levitical laws forbade contact with lepers, dead bodies, anyone bleeding, or anything else that was deemed "unclean." In the New Testament, not only did Jesus touch all these kinds of people, He made them whole. Through grace, the unclean becomes clean.

The Pharisees prayed daily, "God, I thank You that I was not born a Gentile, a slave, or a woman." Paul, the Pharisee of the Pharisees, wrote "there is neither Jew nor Greek, slave nor free, male nor female, for you are all one in Christ Jesus." Grace makes us all equal before God.

In the Old Testament, God says He will *"by no means clear the guilty"* (Exodus 34:7). In the New Testament, God says, *"Their sins and their lawless deeds I will remember no more"* (Hebrews 10:17).

On Mount Sinai, 3,000 people died (Exodus 32:28). After Calvary, on the day of Pentecost, 3,000 people were saved (Acts 2:41). For the Jews, Pentecost is still tied to the Jewish harvest festival of

Shavuot, which celebrates the giving of the Ten Commandments to Moses. For Christians, Pentecost is a celebration of the coming of the Holy Spirit.

The final word in the Old Testament is *"curse"* (Malachi 4:6). But the last thought in the New Testament is, *"The grace of our Lord Jesus Christ be with you all"* (Revelation 22:21).

Which Mountain Do You Live On?

Are you living on Mount Sinai or on Calvary? Are you a disciple of Jesus or a disciple of Moses? In the story of Jesus healing the blind man on the Sabbath (John 9), the Pharisees called themselves the disciples of Moses; the blind man who received his sight became the disciple of Jesus. The disciples of Moses denied the grace of God, but the disciples of Jesus received the grace of God. I want to be a disciple of Jesus.

It's a pretty difficult thing to stand on top of two mountains. We weren't made for that kind of stretching. Once when He was teaching about money, Jesus said that it was impossible to serve two masters. The same is true about the Law and grace, about Mount Sinai and Calvary. You can't serve them both; you can't stand on both. You can only choose one.

So I'll cherish the old rugged cross
Till my trophies at last I lay down;
I will cling to the old rugged cross
And exchange it some day for a crown.

I want to live on Mount Calvary. What about you?

ROUND 4

Going the Distance, Fighting the Confusion

ROUND 4

Another round begins. Grace comes out strong. With cornermen like Paul and James, it seems like Grace has a pretty good chance of putting it away.

But The Law is resilient. He's still got a few shots to throw of his own—and throw them he does, one after the other-- one round after another. Round 4, 5, 6, 7…

The Law gets mouthy too, and starts calling the shots like he's the referee in the boxing ring.

When Grace lands a good cross, The Law calls out, "Not fair!" And when he gets sucker punched, The Law complains, "Low blow!"

As the rounds go deeper, The Law gets noisier and more insolent. But Grace doesn't take the bait. She remembers her coaching, rolls with the punches, and keeps her cool. "Dance like a butterfly, sting like a bee."

Chapter Thirteen:

WHAT GRACE IS NOT

Part of the ongoing and heated debate surrounding grace has to do with the fact that there is a lot of confusion about grace. What is grace? This is a question that people are still wrestling with. One way to understand what grace *is* would be to examine what it *is not*.

1. Grace is not fair.

I have been a Christian almost my entire life. I have faithfully served God since I was a child. But in God's eyes, I look exactly the same as the smoking, drinking, cussing, drug addict who just got saved five minutes ago. When we get to heaven, we will both be dressed in the same white robes of righteousness.

It does not seem fair. I have given my life for God, led over a million people to Jesus, sacrificed on His behalf, and strived to live a holy life. Yet, a man who has thrown his life away in sin and depravity will be given the same reward I receive.

In Matthew 20:1-14, Jesus told a parable about a landowner who hired laborers to work in his vineyard. As the day progressed, he hired more laborers. One hour before sundown, the landowner went to the marketplace and hired another group of laborers. The landowner paid those who only worked for one hour the same amount that he paid those who worked all day. Both received a full day's wages.

There is nothing fair about grace. That's the point. Grace is not fair. None of us deserve grace.

2. Grace is not cheap.

Grace cannot be earned or it's not grace anymore. Besides, who could afford the great price of grace?

Dietrich Bonhoeffer compares cheap grace (grace without a price) with costly grace (grace that cost the blood of God's Son). He writes, "Cheap grace is the grace we bestow on ourselves. Cheap grace is the preaching of forgiveness without requiring repentance, baptism without church discipline, communion without confession.... Cheap grace is grace without discipleship, grace without the cross, grace without Jesus Christ, living and incarnate."

Some have accused grace preachers of preaching a message of "easy forgiveness" or "cheap grace." However, grace is not cheap. Grace cost God His only Son. Grace cost Jesus His life. Grace was so expensive it took the lifeblood of a Savior to pay for it. Paul did not preach "cheap grace." He preached the gospel of grace. We are to preach the Gospel that Paul preached.

3. Grace is not about doing.

What do you have to do to go to heaven? Do you have to be baptized? Do you have to read your Bible every day? Do you have to go to church every Sunday?

Let's ask the thief on the cross next to Jesus. He simply said to Jesus, "Remember me." In the next moment Jesus promised him, "Today you will be with Me in Paradise." The thief had no time to make restitution to those he had wronged, no time for water baptism, no time to live a Christian life; all he did was cry out to Jesus and he was saved.

I often ask people, "What do you have to do to get to heaven?" Most people mumble something about "being good." But, according to Jesus, getting into heaven is not about being good. Getting into heaven is about crying out for help.

Religion always tells you to "Do, do, do..." but Jesus says, "Done, done, done." On the cross, Jesus proclaimed, "It is finished!" He did not say, "To be continued...by someone else."

Religion always tries to "do." The Israelites foolishly told Moses, *"All that the LORD has spoken we will do"* (Exodus 19:8). But, for the entire 1,500 years from Moses to Jesus, not a single Israelite managed to fulfill this promise. They tried with all their might to do what the Law commanded them to do, but not one of them was able to actually keep the Law. Within a mere forty days of making this promise, the children of Israel begged Aaron to make a golden calf for them to worship. God told them not to make idols; they promised to obey, but immediately turned around and built themselves an idol.

The same thing happens today. Every time someone tries to do what the Law commands, they mess up. If you teach the Law, people will look holy on the outside, but not on the inside. The Law is all about us doing something to get something from God.

The most common question people ask me when I talk about my evangelism efforts is, "How do you disciple new believers?"—meaning, "How do you make new converts do what it is that a Christian is supposed to do?" Simply by asking this question, people show that there is a distrust of the concept of grace. God's saving grace is not enough; new converts have to prove they are worthy of heaven by looking and acting like proper Christians. The Bible says, *"Whoever calls on the name of the Lord shall be saved"* (Acts 2:21). Grace means you call on Jesus, period. It does not mean you have to "do" anything. Salvation is so simple that a man driving a speeding car over the edge of a cliff can be saved before he hits the ground by crying out, "Jesus!"

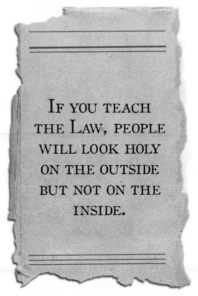

IF YOU TEACH THE LAW, PEOPLE WILL LOOK HOLY ON THE OUTSIDE BUT NOT ON THE INSIDE.

4. Grace is not a reward.

A reward only comes for a good deed. Grace is given, not because of something you have done; it is given because of something Jesus has done.

Grace always upsets religious people. Why? Because then all the things they do (and tell others to do) don't matter anymore— suddenly they are no better than you and they have no power over you.

Our own efforts can never get us to heaven. The problem with religion is that you will never be good enough through your own efforts to make it to heaven. No matter how good you are, your personal best is not good enough.

Once, two men had a jumping contest. One was an Olympic champion of the long jump who was in perfect shape. The other was an obese man who huffed and puffed just walking across the living room. They decided to have a contest to determine who could jump across the Grand Canyon.

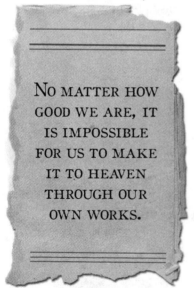

NO MATTER HOW GOOD WE ARE, IT IS IMPOSSIBLE FOR US TO MAKE IT TO HEAVEN THROUGH OUR OWN WORKS.

The obese man could barely run. He waddled up to the edge of the cliff, leaned forward, and managed to jump two feet. He fell to his death at the bottom of the canyon.

Next, the Olympic gold medalist long jumper warmed up and ran as fast as he could at the gaping canyon. He jumped over thirty feet...but unfortunately, he ended up at the same place as the first man: the bottom of the canyon.

No matter how good we are, it is impossible for us to make it to heaven through our own works. The world's most religious man and the world's worst sinner both end up in the pits of hell without accepting Christ's help. You are not justified by your works; you are justified by Christ's work on the cross.

5. Grace is not based on performance.

As a teenager, I did clown shows for children. I dressed in a silly costume, put on clown makeup, rode a unicycle, and juggled. I worked really hard on becoming a good juggler. I practiced for several hours every day. My goal was to have a perfect show without dropping a ball. But no matter how hard I tried and how well I did in practice, I never gave a perfect performance. A light would shine in my eyes, a crying baby would distract me, a breeze would suddenly blow—and I would drop a ball. It was frustrating to try so hard and always fail.

Real life works the same way. Each of us is trying to keep a dozen balls up in the air. We attempt to look good for our audience by putting on a perfect performance. But inevitably, we make a mistake and drop the ball. The truth is that no matter how hard we try, none of us can ever be perfect.

The world puts such a high premium on performance. The majority of human experience teaches us that performance is rewarded. From an early age, we are taught that you get what you deserve, that there is no such thing as a free lunch, that with no pain there is no gain, that the early bird gets the worm, that you earn your living, that you work hard to make it in life. In school, we learn that if we do well on a test we will get an A instead of an F. At our job, we are hired and promoted based on our performance. Even marriage often rises and falls on performance. Instinctively, we feel we must do something in order to receive something.

Humans have an innate desire to figure out how to achieve success. Self-help books give us lists of steps that will help us succeed. We think if we work hard enough, we will be successful.

That is why grace can be hard for us to mentally grasp. Grace is freely given. The whole point of grace is that we do not have to perform in order to get the reward of salvation. Jesus did the perfect performance. As soon as we try to do something to earn our place in heaven, we make grace null and void in our lives. Grace is not based on self-help; grace is based on God's help. Performance is all about what we achieve, but grace is about what we receive.

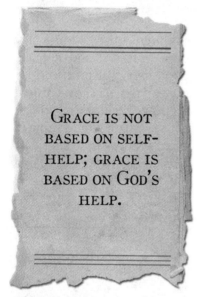

GRACE IS NOT BASED ON SELF-HELP; GRACE IS BASED ON GOD'S HELP.

We often try to earn God's blessings through our efforts. However, there is nothing we can do to earn God's blessing. When we become a Christian, we are made righteous. Once we become righteous, we cannot become more or less righteous. We are either in right standing with God or we are not. Philip Yancey says, "There is nothing we can do to make God love us more. There is nothing we can do to make God love us less." What we do, or do not do, does not influence how God sees us.

Trusting in our own performance is like running on a treadmill that keeps going faster. No matter how much we do or how fast we run, there is always more that we have to do. It's time to get off the gerbil wheel of perfectionism, the treadmill of holiness, the merry-go-round of legalism, and the roller-coaster of sin and repentance.

The heart of every religion is performance. Our performance never impresses God. Our personal best is not good enough. It is such a temptation to fall back into legalism. Our flesh wants to do something to earn God's attention and approval. We need to bring ourselves back to the realization that everything in God's kingdom works by grace.

The spiritual disciplines of religion are like a great rock on your back forcing you to take every step with toil and trouble. But, once you have a revelation of grace, your walk with God becomes a stroll through the park, hand in hand with your Heavenly Father, skipping and laughing together.

6. Grace is not earned.

God does not need you to do anything to earn His love. You are responsible for only one thing, to put your faith in Jesus. Even in this area, God offers His help by giving a measure of faith to every person (Romans 12:3). Soren Kierkegaard writes that the Christian receives "everything by God's grace-grace also. He understands that even in order to pray for is grace he cannot do without God's grace."

A newly born-again believer is often full of excitement. Every day is a new adventure learning to walk and talk with God. But as the new believer goes to church, he often begins to accumulate a long list of do's and don'ts. Gradually, he stops enjoying life with Christ and puts his focus on earning God's love. He is like the church in Revelation who lost their first love.

Once you are saved, in God's eyes you are holy, perfect, righteous, nothing lacking, completely worthy of entrance into the kingdom of heaven. When God looks at you, He does not see you in your human frailty; He sees Jesus. So, if you are completely righteous and completely perfect in God's eyes from salvation onward, what more is your good behavior earning you in terms of salvation?

7. Grace is not a license to sin.

This final point is so important that I am going to dedicate the entire next chapter to talk about it.

Chapter Fourteen:
A LICENSE TO SIN?
Grace in Jude

Many activities in life involve receiving a license. We need a license to drive, a license to get married, a license to hunt, a license to fish, and a license to fly an airplane. At a certain age, it is legal to drink alcohol and buy cigarettes. But before a person turns twenty-one, society says he is too young to drink alcohol. In the same way, the Law was provided for a period of training. However, once you grow up, you no longer need the Law. You get a license—Grace!

A license to fly is not a license to crash your plane. A license for firearms is not a license to shoot out street lights. Being of age to drink, doesn't mean you should be getting drunk. Having a driver's license doesn't make stunt driving legal. So does the license of grace give us the freedom to sin?

The question must be asked. Does the gospel of grace lead to lawlessness? "Antinomianism" is a word originally coined by Martin Luther during the Reformation to describe those who live in lawlessness or are against the Law. The word is made up of two Greek words, *anti* which means "against," and *nomos*, which means "law."

For every mile of road, there are two miles of ditch. On one side of the grace road lies legalism; on the other side of the road are those who see grace as an excuse to sin. And that is the major criticism of the grace message. Grace is being used as an excuse, a license, and a reason to sin.

- A friend of mine interned at a church where the pastor took his entire staff to a local bar and bought them all alcohol just to prove they were under grace.

- I recently heard a television preacher excuse his adultery by saying he was living under God's grace.

- Another preacher decided it was acceptable to watch pornography on his computer because God was "going to forgive him."

- The son of a well-known preacher published a book about grace that supports homosexual "marriage."

Does Grace Allow Us to Sin?

Grace preachers are often accused of allowing people to sin. This accusation is absolutely false. No one who truly preaches grace is saying that it is all right to sin or do wrong. Yet, the accusations continue. Even Paul was accused of encouraging people to sin. You are not really preaching grace until you face the same accusations Paul encountered.

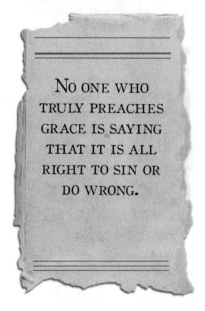

NO ONE WHO TRULY PREACHES GRACE IS SAYING THAT IT IS ALL RIGHT TO SIN OR DO WRONG.

Look how Paul responded to these accusations. He brought balance to the issue by emphasizing that he was not condoning a sinful lifestyle: *"What shall we say then? Shall we continue in sin that grace may abound? Certainly not! How shall we who died to sin live any longer in it?"* (Romans 6:1-2). Paul continues, *"Therefore do not let sin reign in your mortal body, that you should obey it in its lusts...For sin shall not have dominion over you, for you are not under law but under grace"* (Romans 6:12-14). Paul goes on to repeat his original assertion: *"What then? Shall we sin because we are not under law but under grace? Certainly not!"* (Romans 6:15). In the letter to the Galatians he sings the same tune: *"For you, brethren, have been called to liberty; only do not use liberty as an opportunity for the flesh"* (Galatians 5:13).

Charles Spurgeon preached,

> Straightway the unrenewed man seeks out artillery with which to fight against the gospel of the grace of God, and one of the biggest guns he has ever brought to the front is the declaration that the doctrine of the grace of God must lead to licentiousness...This is the constantly-repeated objection which I have heard till it wearies me with its vain and false noise. I am almost ashamed to have to refute so rotten an argument. They dare to assert that men will take license to be guilty because God is gracious, and they do not hesitate to say that if men are not to be saved by their works they will come to the conclusion that their conduct is a matter of indifference, and that they may as well sin that grace may abound...I have admitted that a few human beings have turned the grace of God into lasciviousness; but I trust no one will ever argue against any doctrine on account of the perverse use made of it by the baser sort. Cannot every truth be perverted? ...If we are to condemn a truth because of the misbehavior of individuals who profess to believe it, we should be found condemning our Lord Himself for what Judas did, and our holy faith would die at the hands of apostates and hypocrites. Let us act like rational men. We do not find fault with ropes because poor insane creatures have hanged themselves therewith; nor do we ask that the wares of Sheffield may be destroyed because edged tools are the murderer's instruments.

Sin Is Wrong

Paul was emphatic about grace not giving believers the right to sin. And I stand with Paul. If anything on the foregoing pages of this book has left it unclear, let me clarify any possible misconception regarding my own view of sin: I am absolutely, completely, unequivocally, adamantly, opposed to sin. It is wrong to break God's Law—and that is what sin is. Nothing I say in this book should be used as an excuse for sin.

Why Should We Avoid Sin?

There are several reasons why we should avoid sin.

1. Sin has consequences. The eternal law of sowing and reaping still applies, even to those who have been forgiven. If you sow sin, you will reap destruction in your life. Even if you are forgiven in the eyes of God, here on this earth, sin will destroy you. Grace forgives our sin, but grace does not change the negative consequences that sin can have.

2. Sin opens a door to the devil. This is why Ananias and Sapphira died (Acts 5). They did not die because God judged them; they died because their lie opened a door for Satan to work in their lives. Every problem you have in life is attached to sin; either your sin, Adam's sin, or someone else's sin. Sin is always devastating.

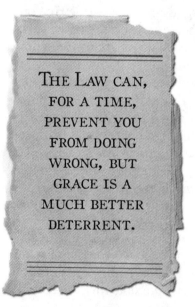

THE LAW CAN, FOR A TIME, PREVENT YOU FROM DOING WRONG, BUT GRACE IS A MUCH BETTER DETERRENT.

3. Sin changes the direction your life is headed. Stephen Hofer says, "Grace doesn't keep us from the destructive results of sin. Sin damages the heart. It makes it difficult to trust God in the future. It makes us doubt God's love and ability to forgive us. When we sin, God does not change and withdraw from us, but in our hearts we change and withdraw from Him." The direction you are headed in reveals your final destination.

Sinning does not make God run away from you; rather it makes you run away from God. Under grace, you have freedom to sin. But walking in sin will pull you away from your relationship with God with no guarantee that you will ever be able to make your way back to Him.

4. Sin enslaves you. Sin actually takes you captive and turns you into a slave. You do not exercise your freedom by sinning; you actually destroy your freedom by sinning.

5. God hates sin. God abhors sin. He cannot allow sin to exist in His presence. The purpose of grace is not to allow sin, but to destroy sin. God's grace empowers you to live holy. God's grace frees you from sin.

Preaching Grace vs. Preaching the Law

Many pastors are afraid of the grace message. They feel that if you tell people that nothing they can do would make God love them less, people will use grace as an excuse to go out and live a life full of sin. Preachers say, "Grace is no license to sin," but I like to say, "Fear of sin is no license to stop preaching grace." The last time I checked, the whole world is already sinning without a license. Preaching the Law does not keep man from sin, because the Law has no power over sin. The Law reveals sin, but does not cure it.

One pastor told me, "If I thought I was free from the Law, people would be horrified at the things I would do." He felt like the only thing keeping him from doing wrong was the Law. The problem with this man's way of thinking is that the Law is a leash that only works for so long.

Imagine a vicious dog. He wants to bite you, but the leash around his neck stops him. If the leash breaks, watch out! However, the same dog will allow his owner to pet him. In fact, the dog turns over and presents his soft belly to be scratched. Why? Because the dog loves his master. The Law can, for a time, prevent you from doing wrong, but grace is a much better deterrent. The pastor I referred to had a heart problem, not a grace problem. Grace, properly preached, actually gives us the heart desire to do what is right.

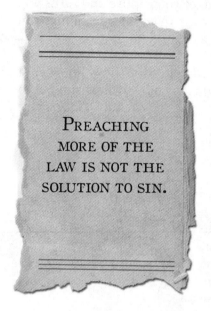

PREACHING MORE OF THE LAW IS NOT THE SOLUTION TO SIN.

The more time you spend with Jesus, the more you want to do what is right. Imagine what would happen if Jesus was physically present with you in your everyday life? If He was walking beside you at the grocery store, would you be tempted to shoplift? Would being with Jesus make you want to cheat on your spouse? No!

Look at what happened when Zacchaeus encountered Jesus. He promised to make restitution to all those he had stolen from. Being with Jesus made him a better person. The more grace you experience, the better you will live your life. Grace is not an excuse for you to sin; grace is actually the motivation that keeps you from sinning.

Under grace, you can do anything you "want to." However, grace gives you a new "want to." You are not free to do whatever you please, you are free to please God. As Paul said, *"All things are lawful for me, but not all things are helpful; all things are lawful for me, but not all things edify"* (1 Corinthians 10:23).

Preaching more of the Law is not the solution to sin. Many preachers who have preached the Law the strongest have been caught sinning themselves. The solution to sin is to preach more grace. The more people know about Jesus, the less likely they are to sin.

Preaching grace makes people want to stay away from sin. When you know that you are righteous, the desire to sin disappears. The more righteousness-conscious you are, the less you will want to sin. When righteousness is preached correctly, it motivates people to live better lives. As Paul said, *"Awake to righteousness, and do not sin"* (1 Corinthians 15:34).

People who have truly been touched by grace no longer want to sin. It is like a man who has broken his leg. Just because he finds a doctor who can heal his broken leg does not mean that he rushes out to break it again. Instead, he remembers the pain he felt when it was broken. Grace is the heart of the Christian message. If you stop preaching grace because you are scared of sin, you have missed the entire point of the good news.

Sin and the Grace Message in Jude

The tendency to use grace as an excuse for sin is nothing new—it was an issue for the early Church as much as for the Church today. Jude, a leader in the early Church, addressed this concern. Let's look at his book for wisdom and understanding of this issue.

Jude begins by writing, *"Beloved, while I was very diligent to write to you concerning our common salvation, I found it necessary to write to you exhorting you to contend earnestly for the faith which was once for all delivered to the saints"* (Jude 1:3). In this passage, Jude is asking the beloved (those who believe) to contend earnestly for their original faith. What is your original faith? It was the point when you realized that you were a sinner in need of a Savior. It was when you bowed your knee before Christ and made Him Lord of your life. Go back to the original faith and say, "Jesus is my Lord."

Jude continues, *"For certain men have crept in unnoticed, who long ago were marked out for this condemnation, ungodly men, who turn the grace of our God into lewdness and deny the only Lord God and our Lord Jesus Christ"* (Jude 1:4). Jude warns us that the day is coming when people will use grace as an excuse for lewdness. What is "lewdness?" Lewdness is lust, perversion, uncleanness, and uncontrolled sin. Jude warns there will come a time when people will say:

- Because grace has come, I am free to sin in any way I want to.

- I will make it to heaven, even if I live like the devil.

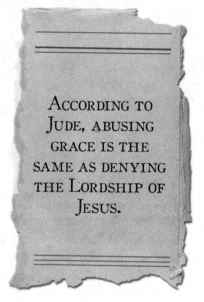

ACCORDING TO JUDE, ABUSING GRACE IS THE SAME AS DENYING THE LORDSHIP OF JESUS.

- I can do anything I want.

- No more laws, no more legalism; I am free to enjoy all kinds of sin and still be saved.

- I can confess Jesus and continue to do the same sinful things.

- I like the promises of divine blessing; I like the music at church; I like the fellowship on Sunday, but I don't want to change the way I live my life the other six days of the week.

What's wrong with these statements? Grace changes your heart. If the grace of God changes your heart, then the grace of God will change and affect your actions and lifestyle too. One proverb says, *"Out of the heart flow the issues of life"* (Proverbs 4:23). When grace is in your heart, it will issue out into your life too.

Jude calls those who treat the grace of God as license for sin "ungodly men," and charges them with denying "the only Lord God and our Lord Jesus Christ." According to Jude, abusing grace is the same as denying the lordship of Jesus.

Jude's Three Illustrations of the Consequences of Sin

Jude goes on to illustrate the consequences of using grace as a license for sin, giving us three examples from the Old Testament.

1. The children of Israel in the desert were saved from Egypt through grace, but because of their sin, they brought destruction upon their lives. *"But I want to remind you, though you once knew this, that the Lord, having saved the people out of the land of Egypt, afterward destroyed those who did not believe"* (Jude 1:5).

2. The angels in heaven rebelled against God and earned eternal damnation. *"And the angels who did not keep their proper domain, but left their own abode, He has reserved in everlasting chains under darkness for the judgment of the great day"* (Jude 1:6). James offers us some good commentary on Jude's passage: *"You believe that there is one God. You do well. Even the demons believe and tremble!"* (James 2:19). Even the demons believe, but they do not submit to God's lordship. The belief produces no change in the demons. You can't say, "I'm a believer," keep on sinning, and expect to make it to heaven. For demons, right believing does not lead to right living.

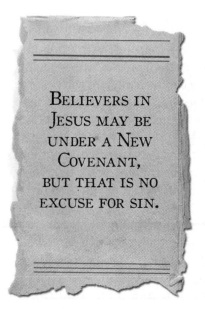

BELIEVERS IN JESUS MAY BE UNDER A NEW COVENANT, BUT THAT IS NO EXCUSE FOR SIN.

3. Sodom and Gomorrah engaged in wickedness and were wiped from the face of the earth. *"As Sodom and Gomorrah, and the cities around them in a similar manner to these, having given themselves over to sexual immorality and gone after strange flesh, are set forth as an example, suffering the vengeance of eternal fire"* (Jude 1:7).

Jude warns the New Covenant believer through three Old Covenant illustrations of the danger and consequences of abusing the grace of God. Believers in Jesus may be under a New Covenant, but that is no excuse for sin.

The erroneous teaching that grace gives us freedom to sin is a slippery slope. Saying you don't have to live for God because of His grace is only one step away from the heretical idea of universal salvation that says everyone on earth will go to heaven because of His grace, regardless of whether they ever made Jesus their Lord. If it is true that a person can continue in sin and still be under God's grace, I still lose nothing by living righteously. However, if it is true that God's grace compels you to live a holy life, and you choose to continue in sin, then you will suffer eternal consequences.

Walking In Grace Requires Humility

"Be clothed with humility," writes the Apostle Peter, *"for God resists the proud, but gives grace to the humble. Therefore humble yourselves under the mighty hand of God, that He may exalt you in due time… Be sober, be vigilant; because your adversary the devil walks about like a roaring lion, seeking whom he may devour. Resist him, steadfast in the faith"* (1 Peter 5:5-6, 8-9).

The root of sin is pride. Lucifer tried to become like God and fell from heaven. Now he goes about seeking to bring destruction into the lives of believers. The serpent tempted Adam and Eve by saying, "If you eat the fruit, you will become like God." Cain killed Abel because of pride. It is pride that says, "Grace allows me to do anything I want to do without repentance and without a change." There is grace and there is forgiveness, but it comes on God's conditions, not yours. The psalmist wrote: "But there is forgiveness with You, that You may be feared" (Psalm 130:4). God's conditions include genuine faith that changes your heart, your mind, your words, and every part of your being and lifestyle. Grace does not lead you into disobedience, but into obedience.

HUMILITY IS RECOGNIZING THAT GOD IS THE SOURCE OF EVERYTHING THAT YOU HAVE AND NEED.

Pride makes you want to put Jesus down and make yourself lord. Pride turns away from God because it says you do not need Him. Walking in grace requires humbleness because you can no longer boast in your own abilities; instead, you have to completely rely on what Christ has done for you. You must come to God empty-handed. Humility is recognizing that God is the Source of everything that you have and need.

The story of the prodigal son is a powerful illustration of the truth of how humility enables us to experience God's grace. The youngest son certainly abused his father's grace—demanding his portion of the inheritance was effectively saying he wished his father was dead. Then the son went out and wasted this wealth in riotous living. After he lost everything and was living with pigs, he remembered his father: *"he came to himself"* (Luke 15:17).

He realized he was not in the right place. His father was far away while he was living with the pigs. His father's servants lived a lot better than he did. Before you can receive God's grace, you have to realize that you need God's grace. Stop living in sin and return to your Father.

The son said, *"I will arise and go to my father, and will say to him, 'Father, I have sinned against heaven and before you, and I am no longer worthy to be called your son. Make me like one of your hired servants'"* (Luke 15:18-19). He humbled himself before his father and repented.

Genuine faith confesses sin; it does not hide it or apologize for it. Faith repents of sin. The son humbled himself and knelt before his father. Of course, the father received him with grace. *"When he was still a great way off, his father saw him and had compassion, and ran and fell on his neck and kissed him"* (Luke 15:20). Your Father is not mad at you, He is ready to receive you and welcome you home.

The father rejoiced, *"My son was dead and is alive again; he was lost and is found"* (Luke 15:24). The son was spiritually dead. His father's love and grace never stopped, but when the son walked away, the relationship died. God's grace is always available and His forgiveness is always there, but if we are away from God, enjoying riotous living, we will be dead to Him.

GRACE IS THE ABILITY TO RUN AWAY FROM SIN.

The son arose, returned, confessed, and repented. The son humbled himself and the father lifted him up and gave him a robe of righteousness, a ring of authority, sandals that meant he was family, and a fatted calf which represented provision. If you have been living in sin, go back to your Father. Humble yourself and let God raise you up. Go back to the original faith that got you saved when you first believed in Jesus and surrendered to Him, making Him Lord of your life.

Grace Empowers You to Live a Holy Life.

How did Jesus live a sinless life? He was fully God, but He was also fully man. It was as a human that He resisted temptation. The temptation He faced was the same as the temptations we face today. Jesus *"was in all points tempted as we are, yet without sin"* (Hebrews 4:15).

So how can we resist the human desire to sin? The answer is found in the next verse, *"Let us therefore come boldly to the throne of grace, that we may obtain mercy and find grace to help in time of need"* (Hebrews 4:16). It was at the feet of His Father that Jesus found the ability to resist temptation. God's grace helps us overcome temptation. By the way, what is the difference between grace and mercy? Grace is receiving from God that which we do not deserve (reward). Mercy is not receiving from God that which we do deserve (punishment).

Grace does not permit sin, but it does stand ready to forgive it. Even if you make a mistake, God still loves you. However, grace is far more than a way to cover up sin. Grace actually gives us the power to resist sin. Grace is not an excuse to get away with sinning. Grace is the ability to run away from sin. It is not our ability that enables us to resist temptation; it is His ability working in us.

Imagine the Super Bowl is being played in your hometown. You have been a die-hard football fan your entire life and your greatest dream is to attend the big game. The only problem is, you do not have enough money for a ticket. In fact, your family is so poor the most you can scrape together through your own efforts is two dollars. For weeks, you try to bid for a ticket on the Internet. You keep bidding your $2, but scalpers are selling the tickets for $2,000.

Miraculously, the owner of one of the teams hears about your situation. Generously, he gives you, free of charge, a ticket to sit in the skybox with his family. Not only will you have the best seat in the house, but you are also entitled to all the free food and drinks you want.

GRACE IS YOUR TICKET INTO HEAVEN. YOUR ENTRANCE FEE HAS BEEN COMPLETELY PAID BY JESUS CHRIST.

To celebrate, you decide to throw the best tailgate party ever. As you drive onto the stadium grounds, you see a big sign with some rules. It says, "No fighting, no cussing, no roughhousing, no open fires." You are not worried about the rules because you have a ticket.

Your tailgate party gets out of hand. You start an open fire next to your truck to cook hotdogs. A fight breaks out with fans from a rival team. Security is called. Because the rules have been broken, they decide to eject you from the stadium grounds. You protest, "But I have a ticket!" A security guard explains, "Sir, having a ticket to get into the game does not mean you have the freedom to do whatever you like. You still have to follow the rules."

Grace is your ticket into heaven. Your entrance fee has been completely paid by Jesus Christ. You are completely unable to earn your way into heaven through your own efforts. Your ticket into heaven is a free gift. But, having a ticket to get into heaven does not mean you can live any way you want to live. God still gives us instructions and guidelines for how we should live our lives here on the earth. Grace does not give you permission to sin; instead it motivates you to keep the highest standards in your life.

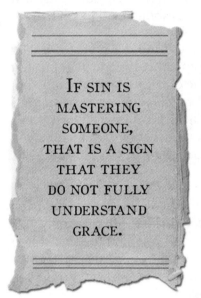

IF SIN IS MASTERING SOMEONE, THAT IS A SIGN THAT THEY DO NOT FULLY UNDERSTAND GRACE.

Why Do People Covered By Grace Still Sin?

If our "old man" is dead, why do we still sin? Paul wrote, "*But now, it is no longer I who do it, but sin that dwells in me…Now if I do what I will not to do, it is no longer I who do it, but sin that dwells in me*" (Romans 7:17, 20). Paul says, "We died to sin, how can we live in it any longer?" Sin is part of the old man that is now dead. Why would anyone want to walk around with a stinking, decaying corpse strapped to his back? But that is what it is like when we sin—we carry around the dead "old man" with us. It's a heavy burden.

Unfortunately, the only time many pastors emphasize grace is after they themselves have done something wrong. Suddenly, they start using grace to excuse their own failings. Because of this, there has been a lot of criticism of the "radical grace" or "hyper-grace" message.

Sin is a symptom. If sin is mastering someone, that is a sign that they do not fully understand grace. If you know how to cook but never cook, what use is it to you? If you understand the love of Christ but never let it change you, then what is the point of knowing about the love of Christ? The solution to sin is to hear more about grace and more about Jesus. The more time one spends with Jesus, the less one wants to sin.

How to Handle Sin

So, what should our response be to those who are under grace, maybe even preaching grace, but are still living sinful lives?

1. Have mercy, because you could fall yourself. *"Brothers, if someone is caught in a sin, you who are spiritual should restore him gently. But watch yourself, or you also may be tempted"* (Galatians 6:1). *"Therefore let him who thinks he stands take heed lest he fall"* (1 Corinthians 10:12).

2. Continue to preach grace. I do not stop driving my car because someone had a car wreck. The abuse of grace is no reason to stop preaching grace. We should show grace even to those preachers who preach about grace and continue to sin. Just because someone preaches on grace does not mean that they fully understand it or are walking in it completely.

The power of sin is the Law. *"The sting of death is sin, and the strength of sin is the law"* (1 Corinthians 15:56). If someone warns you to watch out for "grace preachers" because they give people a "license to sin," remind them that Paul said that the strength of sin is the Law. It is not the preaching of grace that empowers sinful behavior; rather, it is the preaching of the Law.

3. Don't judge. As Christians, we are called to, "Love the sinner; hate the sin." Bob Stamps says, "God is not against you for your sins; He is for you against your sins." Jesus advised us not to pull up weeds lest we pull up the wheat too (Matthew 13:29). Our job is not to judge who is a weed and who is wheat, our job is to continue to plant the seed of God's Word in as many hearts as we can. Don't judge those who break the Law—that is God's job. *"Do not speak evil of one another, brethren. He who speaks evil of a brother and* *judges his brother, speaks evil of the law and judges the law. But if you judge the law, you are not a doer of the law but a judge. There is one Lawgiver, who is able to save and to destroy. Who are you to judge another?"* (James 4:11-12).

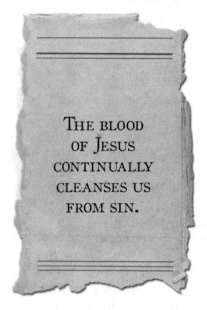

THE BLOOD OF JESUS CONTINUALLY CLEANSES US FROM SIN.

What does it mean when Christians say that God "loves the sinner but hates the sin"? It is like having a shiny new car and being angry that it has a scratch in the side. The new car owner is willing to pay a great price to get the scratch fixed. He's not mad at the vehicle; he's mad at the scratch, the flaw that disfigured his beautiful car. The wrath of God is founded in the love of God because He hates it when His creations are defaced. He loves us so much that He is upset at our flaws. It because of His love that He offers a solution to help us become whole.

4. Continue to love those who sin. Jesus had a reputation of being "a friend of sinners." Have you sinned in thought, word, or deed today? The truth is that everyone sins (1 Kings 8:46; Psalm 14:2-3; Psalm 51:5; Proverbs 21:4; Proverbs 24:9; Romans 3:10-12). Most people sin twenty times before they finish breakfast.

But the good news is that the blood of Jesus washes away our sins. *"The blood of Jesus Christ His Son cleanses us from all sin"* (1 John 1:7). The Greek word for "cleanse" is in the continuous present tense. This means that the blood of Jesus continually cleanses us from sin. It is not a one-time event, it is a continuous waterfall of forgiveness continuing to cleanse us every time we sin again. *"Jesus took the iniquity of us all"* (Isaiah 53:6). That's good news!

Chapter Fifteen:

GOD'S JUDGMENT

Is God judging North America? Is God angry with you? Is He about to hit you with a lightning bolt? Or is He a loving God who is full of mercy and forgiveness?

Many Christians seem schizophrenic when it comes to what they think and believe about God. One day they preach that God is mad at you, and the next day they say, "Jesus loves you." One day the Almighty is judging you; the next day He gives you mercy. One minute, He is smiling at you; the next minute, He is frowning at you. This schizophrenia produces two kinds of Christians: those who think you should get Jesus, and those who think Jesus is going to get you!

When the tsunami hit South Asia in 2004, some Christians said it was God's judgment upon the heathen in that part of the world. When New Orleans was flooded in 2005, many pastors preached that the flood was a sign of God's wrath for all the wild Mardi Gras parties on Bourbon Street. After the earthquake hit Haiti in 2010, a television preacher said it was a sign of God's anger at the sin of the Haitian people. And doubtless, as fresh disasters visit different corners of our globe, there will be a "Job's comforter" to make similar kinds of remarks on those events too. But if God is so angry at sin, why is Las Vegas still standing?

What makes God angry? If you study the Bible, you will find that only sin makes God angry. But now, because of what Jesus accomplished on the cross, the price for sin has been paid. God is no longer angry.

The truth is that there are three different types of judgment—past, present, and future.

Past Judgment

First, there is a judgment that has happened in the past. This is the judgment for sin that Jesus paid for at the cross. God poured out all of His wrath and anger on Jesus. Since Jesus paid the full price for sin, it never has to be paid for again by anyone who accepts Jesus as Savior. Every sin we have ever committed, or will commit in the future, was put on Jesus at the cross—without exception. All your sins are forgiven. *"And you, being dead in your trespasses and the uncircumcision of your flesh, He has made alive together with Him, having forgiven you all trespasses, having wiped out the handwriting of requirements that was against us, which was contrary to us. And He has taken it out of the way, having nailed it to the cross"* (Colossians 2:13-14).

Present Judgment

Second, there is a chastisement for the present. This is not the type of judgment that an angry judge would dispense, rather it is the discipline of a loving Father. This present chastisement is mentioned in Hebrews 12:7 and Revelation 3:19. The purpose of God's discipline is not to *pay* you back, but to *bring* you back. For example, when Jonah was swallowed by a whale, he felt like he was being punished, but really God was just trying to get him back on track.

Future Judgment

Finally, there is a future judgment at the Judgment Seat of Christ. *"For we must all appear before the judgment seat of Christ, that each one may receive the things done in the body, according to what he has done, whether good or bad"* (2 Corinthians 5:10). Payday is coming, and we will all have to give an account for our actions. At that point, the catalog of your mundane actions are going to be something of vital interest to you. That day is coming, but as long as you are breathing, you can experience God's mercy.

Facts About the Future Judgment

1. When Jesus returns, we will be rewarded for everything we have done on the earth. *"For the Son of Man will come in the glory of His Father with His angels, and then He will reward each according to his works"* (Matthew 16:27).

While the word "rewarded" usually has positive connotations, here it does not have that meaning. Here the word means simply that you will get what is coming to you as a consequence of the things you have done.

2. At the Judgment Seat, our works here on this earth will be judged.

- *"I saw the dead, small and great, standing before God, and books were opened. And another book was opened, which is the Book of Life. And the dead were judged according to their works, by the things which were written in the books. The sea gave up the dead who were in it, and Death and Hades delivered up the dead who were in them. And they were judged, each one according to his works"* (Revelation 20:12-13).

- *"And if you call on the Father, who without partiality judges according to each one's work, conduct yourselves throughout the time of your stay here in fear"* (1 Peter 1:17).

GOD IS ANGRY NO LONGER.

- *"Let us hear the conclusion of the whole matter: Fear God and keep His commandments, for this is man's all. For God will bring every work into judgment, including every secret thing, whether good or evil"* (Ecclesiastes 12:13-14).

Good and evil will be the criteria

that will determine how our works are judged. The epic struggle between good and evil will at last be sorted out. Be assured, God is an impartial Judge. He will not judge unfairly, but His judgments will be found to be justified (Psalm 51:4)

3. God will reward us in heaven for our works.

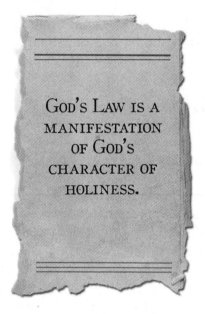

GOD'S LAW IS A MANIFESTATION OF GOD'S CHARACTER OF HOLINESS.

- *"I am coming quickly, and My reward is with Me, to give to every one according to his work"* (Revelation 22:12).

- *"All the churches shall know that I am He who searches the minds and hearts. And I will give to each one of you according to your works"* (Revelation 2:23).

4. Evil deeds will be punished in heaven on the "day of wrath."

- *"But in accordance with your hardness and your impenitent heart you are treasuring up for yourself wrath in the day of wrath and revelation of the righteous judgment of God, who will render to each one according to his deeds"* (Romans 2:5-6).

Wrath, anger, and its consequences will one day be the portion of those who are found to be unrighteous.

God Thinks Outside the Box

Even though there is a future judgment coming, here on this earth God wants to bless you, not punish you. The Ark of the Covenant illustrates this truth. The Ark was the Jews' most cherished possession since it carried the tangible presence of God on earth.

The Ark represented two things that must always be kept in balance: God's holiness and God's mercy.

The Ark was a box built of acacia wood overlaid with gold. According to Exodus 25:10, the Ark was approximately 3.75 feet long, 2.25 feet wide, and 2.25 feet high. Hidden within the box was the stone tablets of the Ten Commandments—the symbol of God's Law.

God's Law is a manifestation of God's character of holiness. Because God loves righteousness, holiness, and truth, the Law is perfect, holy, and just. All who break the Law must be judged as law-breakers in accordance with the Law. Breaking the Law of God is, of course, the essence of sin. While God wants to bless you, He cannot bless sin. Sin must be punished because the Law has been broken. God's holy character demands justice.

The cover of the Ark reveals a second element of God's character. Moses received God's instructions: *"make the Ark's cover, the place of atonement, out of pure gold. It must be 3.75 feet long and 2.25 feet wide"* (Exodus 25:17 NLT). This lid is known as the "Place of Atonement" or "The Mercy Seat."

During Old Testament times, once each year the high priest poured the blood of a goat over this mercy seat (Leviticus 16:15). The goat was a substitute for all the people of Israel and in a ceremony, the Israelites would symbolically place their sins on the goat. The goat was then killed as a sacrifice for the sins of the people. However, there was a problem: this sacrifice was only temporarily effective. Year after year, the death of another goat was needed to atone for the fresh sins of the Israelites.

God wanted to permanently and effectively deal with the issue of sin, so He sent Jesus Christ, the perfect sacrifice, to die once and for all for the sins of humankind (Hebrews 9:28). When Jesus died on the cross, He paid the price for your sin and my sin. Christ's death and resurrection is evidence of God's mercy.

BECAUSE OF CHRIST, GOD'S NEED FOR JUDGMENT IS COMPLETELY COVERED BY GOD'S MERCY.

Under the New Covenant, Jesus becomes our Mercy Seat. Romans 3:25-26 says, "*whom God set forth as a propitiation by His blood, through faith, to demonstrate His righteousness, because in His forbearance God had passed over the sins that were previously committed, to demonstrate at the present time His righteousness, that He might be just and the justifier of the one who has faith in Jesus.*" The word "propitiation" is the Greek word *hilasterion*, a word that can also be translated as "mercy seat."

Now for the best news of all: God says to you, "*I will meet with you, and I will speak with you from above the mercy seat*" (Exodus 25:22). God wants to speak to you, not where the Law is kept, not where judgment is meted out, but in a place of mercy!

Inside the box there is judgment. But notice, the mercy seat is exactly the same size as the ark. Because of Christ, God's need for judgment is completely covered by God's mercy. Outside the box, Jesus poured His blood on the mercy seat of heaven so that all can be saved.

Many preachers stay inside the box. They preach from a place of judgment and condemnation. People become depressed trying to follow an endless list of religious rules. God wants us to think outside the box. All of God's need for judgment was poured out on

Jesus at the cross. God is not judging our nation; God is smiling upon us. Preachers, listen to me. God is not inside the box. He is waiting to meet us at the place of mercy, forgiveness, and love. We should preach mercy, not Law.

Without mercy, no human being could go to heaven. If we try to approach God from inside the box (on the basis of the Law), we would be judged and condemned to an eternity separated from God. But God does not want to meet us at the Law; He desires to meet us at the mercy seat, the place of atonement and forgiveness where *"mercy triumphs over judgment!"* (James 2:13).

This is the difference between religion and a relationship with God. Religion tries to force people to stay inside the box. Religion provides a list of rules and regulations. Religion is about the Law. You can experience a relationship with God not based on rules, but based on the mercy that His grace and love have provided.

Think Outside the Box

Jesus told a parable about two men who went to the temple to pray (Luke 18:9-14). One was a Pharisee, a religious leader. The second was a tax collector. The Pharisee began to pray, "God, I thank You that I am not like other men--robbers, evildoers, adulterers, or even like this tax collector. I fast twice a week and give a tenth of all I have."

The tax collector stood in the corner and would not even look up to heaven; he just beat his breast and said, "God, have mercy on me, a sinner." Jesus said, "I tell you that the tax collector, rather than the Pharisee, went home justified before God."

The Pharisee approached God from within the box (based on Law), but the tax collector approached God at the place of mercy. The tax collector was the one made righteous.

Before we were saved, we were dead in sin. *"But because of His great love for us, God, who is rich in mercy, made us alive with Christ even when we were dead in transgressions"* (Ephesians 2:4-

5). When you die, what will you be placed in? A box? A coffin? Jesus, through His mercy, made us alive. He set us free from the box. It's time to think outside the box!

Chapter Sixteen:

NO CONDEMNATION

Dusk had begun, the shadows lengthening in every corridor. The woman pulled her shawl tightly about her shoulders. She poked her head around the corner of the alley and cautiously looked both ways. Not a soul was in sight. She hastily crossed the street to a wooden door hidden in the shadows. She knocked in anticipation. The door opened softly, strong arms pulled her inside, and she melted into the warm embrace of her young lover.

The woman looked up into his dark eyes as he leaned down with a gentle kiss. She loved this man. He was the son of a Pharisee, tall and handsome. Their relationship began two years ago, when she felt his eyes on her as they left the synagogue. Flustered, she tripped and almost fell. He reached out to steady her, then pulled back before anyone noticed. After that they started to talk. Then they held hands. Then they kissed. Now, she was sneaking into his father's house to spend time with him. She knew it was wrong for them to be together, but it felt so right. Like they had done before, the couple eagerly stripped off their garments and fell into each other's passionate embrace.

Early the next morning, the door slammed opened and woke them. His father was standing there with glaring eyes. "I knew something was going on," he shouted. "You shall be punished."

"Father," wailed the young man.

"Shut up!" yelled the dad. "I'll deal with you later."

He grabbed the woman by her hair and dragged her from the bed—she just managed to grab onto a sheet to cover her nakedness. He pulled her through the house, out into the street and down to the synagogue. Her heart had never beat so fast.

To her shame, a crowd began collecting the whole way down the street, and they now joined those who were already at the synagogue. She hid her face, lest any recognize her. The irate father threw her at the feet of a man who was talking to those who had gathered there earlier.

The Pharisee interrupted Him: "Teacher, this woman was caught in adultery, in the very act of sinning. In the Law, Moses commanded us that she should be stoned. What do You think we should do?" The other Pharisees chanted, "Stone her!"

Several Pharisees began picking up rocks, preparing to throw them at the adulteress. She cowered where she had been shoved and shielded her head. But before they could attack her, the Teacher leaned down and began to write in the dirt. The girl could not see what He was writing. The Pharisees asked again, "Should we stone her?"

The Teacher said, "He who is without sin among you, let him throw the first stone." Then He wrote on the ground some more. Slowly, the roar of the crowd faded as the angry men began to walk away. The last to leave was the Pharisee who had caught her in bed with his son.

She looked up at the face of the Teacher. She recognized Him. It was Jesus. He said to her, "Woman, where are those accusers of yours? Has no one condemned you?"

The woman looked around and then bowed her head, "No one, Lord." Then Jesus lovingly said to her, "Neither do I condemn you; go and sin no more."

The woman left thankful for her life. Because of the grace which she had been shown, she vowed in her heart that never again would she do wrong.

Should We Condemn People or Set Them Free?

Like the adulterous woman, all of us have sinned. We are all guilty. If we break one of God's laws, it is equivalent to breaking all of them. So, sin is a level playing field. None of us have the right to judge another because all of us have made mistakes. We should leave judgment in God's hands—and His judgment was poured out on Jesus at the cross. Jesus did not condemn the woman caught in adultery, nor is He condemning you. Jesus set her free from condemnation before He admonished her not to sin anymore.

Sinners hear a message of judgment over and over again from the church. They know they are doing wrong. But a message of judgment never works to draw people closer to God. Joseph Prince points out that "preaching more of the Law to counteract sin is like adding wood to fire." What people focus on is what they will be. Preach grace and people will be attracted to righteousness. Preach the Law and people will be tempted to sin.

Preaching the Law can be attractive. Some ministers become legalistic because they want to clean up the sheep, and legalism looks like a shortcut to getting the sheep clean. In reality, legalism only makes people look clean temporarily. Grace is far more than outward behavior modification; it is inward transformation.

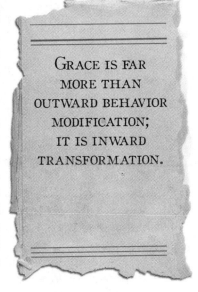

GRACE IS FAR MORE THAN OUTWARD BEHAVIOR MODIFICATION; IT IS INWARD TRANSFORMATION.

Another reason ministers often become legalistic is because they want to control people. Under grace, you can't control people any longer. How does your church make people feel about God? Do they feel set free by God, or do they see God as controlling? Do they feel condemned by God, or do they feel more in love with Him?

The Law Condemns

Once I heard a street minister ask a man who was walking by, "Have you ever lied? Have you ever stolen? Have you ever committed adultery? Before you answer, keep in mind that Jesus said if you even look at a woman lustfully, you are guilty of adultery." The man was forced to answer in the affirmative to each question. The minister continued, "So what does that make you? By your own admission, you are a lying, adulterous thief."

This script produced condemnation, but it did not lead to salvation. Salvation does not come by the Law; it comes through mercy and truth. *"In mercy and truth atonement is provided for iniquity; And by the fear of the LORD one departs from evil"* (Proverbs 16:6).

CONDEMNATION IS SATAN'S GREATEST WEAPON.

You do not have to bash people over the head with the fact that they are on their way to hell. Intuitively, people already know they are sinners. When Adam sinned, he ran to hide from God without God ever saying anything about the forbidden fruit. The threat of God's judgment can make people feel guilty, and may even frighten them into good behavior, but it does not change their heart or free them from sin.

When Jesus is preached, salvation results. Preaching about Jesus makes people want to know God. Romans 2:4 proclaims, *"the goodness of God leads you to repentance."* God uses grace to lead people to repentance. Preaching grace is preaching the power of God unto salvation.

So, if it is the goodness of God that leads men to repentance, why do so many preachers preach condemnation, Law, and judgment? The Ten Commandments *"written and engraved on stone"* are called a *"ministry of death"* and a *"ministry of condemnation"* (2 Corinthians 3:7-9). When ministers preach the Law, they are preaching a death and condemnation.

Satan Is "The Accuser"

Satan is known as "the accuser." He uses the Law to beat you up. He accuses you by saying, "You don't read the Bible enough;" "you don't pray enough;" "you don't give enough." By making these accusations, the accuser is trying to make you feel guilty.

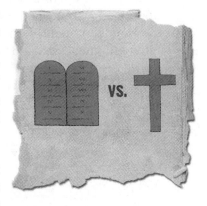

Condemnation is Satan's greatest weapon. The devil wants you to be under the Law—many of his tricks and insidious lies are attempts to convince you to keep the Law. Satan is always trying to pull you back into works-based self-righteousness, because he knows that if you approach God based on your own works, you will be found lacking and feel condemned. When you put yourself under the Law, you put a weapon in Satan's hand. But if you are free of the Law, Satan is out of ammunition all of a sudden. There is no way for Satan to condemn you any longer.

The Most Radical Verse in the Bible

Recently I was invited to share at a Bible study. One man stood up and prophesied that God was about to judge America. He announced, "Because America has allowed abortions, homosexuality, and blatant sexual sins, God is angry at America." He continued, "In Deuteronomy 28, there are five curses for every blessing. If you do not repent, you will be under a curse. Because of America's sin, sickness and poverty will come upon you."

I interrupted him and said, "Sir, all of God's judgment was poured out on Jesus at the cross. Jesus took the curse. God now looks at us through the blood of Jesus. God does not curse us; He looks at us from a place of mercy, love, and forgiveness."

The man was offended at my words, but I continued, "In the Old Testament, we see God's judgment. His wrath burned against the Israelites during the time of Moses. Fire and brimstone rained down on Sodom and Gomorrah. Elijah called down fire from heaven. But in the New Testament, Jesus revealed God as a loving Father. All of God's judgment was poured out on Jesus at the cross. The cross makes all the difference in the world. It is the dividing line between God's judgment and His love."

GOD IS NOT ANGRY ANYMORE!

I finished by turning to the most radical verse in the Bible, *"There is therefore now no condemnation to those who are in Christ Jesus"* (Romans 8:1).

In Old Testament times, God was angry at those who broke the Law. But Jesus redeemed us from the curse of the Law, so God is not angry anymore! God is not mad at America or the world; God is smiling at the world. God is not judging America. God is not judging you. His mercy triumphs over His judgment. God is not up in heaven trying to beat you up; He is in heaven reaching out to you.

Even when people are living in sin, God still loves them and offers them the hope of salvation. We are not sinners in the hands of an angry God; we are sinners in the hands of a merciful God.

Jesus did not come to condemn, curse, or judge the world. Jesus told Nicodemus, *"For God did not send His Son into the world to condemn the world, but that the world through Him might be saved"* (John 3:17).

Why do I call Romans 8:1 the most radical verse in the Bible? Because it completely sets the believer free from condemnation for doing wrong.

On another occasion, right when I was celebrating the fact that "there is no condemnation for those who are in Christ," a holiness preacher quoted the rest of the Scripture to me, "There is no condemnation to those...who do not walk according to the flesh, but according to the Spirit."

"See," he said, "if you walk in the flesh and start sinning, you will be right back under condemnation."

This interpretation bothered me so much that I went and looked up the Scripture in my Greek New Testament. Did you know that this phrase "who do not walk according to the flesh, but according to the Spirit" is not found in the original Greek? So, what is it doing there?

The translators were so blinded by their legalistic theology that they could not believe the verse as it was originally written. Its declaration of freedom was too large, so they added a qualification to the verse. The good news of our absolute freedom in Christ was too radical for those translators to handle. And it is still too radical for many today.

What About the Holy Spirit?

One friend asked, "But doesn't the Holy Spirit convict us of sin?"

"Yes," I had to say, "that's true. But there is a major difference between Satan's condemnation and the Holy Spirit's conviction."

Condemnation tells you how bad you are; conviction tells you how good you can become through Jesus. Condemnation is Satan trying to make you feel guilty. Conviction is the Holy Spirit reminding you that through Jesus, you are righteous and have no need to sin any longer. Condemnation pushes you to desperation; conviction pushes you to repent and rely on Jesus.

Let's look at John 16:8-11, *"And when He [The Comforter] has come, He will convict the world of sin, and of righteousness, and of judgment: of sin, because they do not believe in Me; of righteousness, because I go to My Father and you see Me no more; of judgment, because the ruler of this world is judged."* The Holy Spirit is a Comforter, not a condemner. The Holy Spirit will convict the world of sin (singular), the sin of not believing in Jesus. But for the believer, the Holy Spirit convicts us of righteousness.

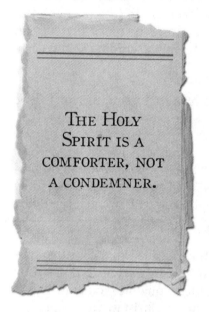

THE HOLY SPIRIT IS A COMFORTER, NOT A CONDEMNER.

When Satan Accuses Us, God Defends Us!

You don't need to be worried about sin, because you have an Advocate: *"If anyone sins, we have an Advocate with the Father, Jesus Christ the righteous"* (1 John 2:1). Jesus is not our only Advocate. The word "Comforter," used by Jesus to refer to the Holy Spirit, also means "Advocate." And what greater picture of advocacy on our behalf is there than of God the Father—giving up His own Son for the sake of sinners. The Father, the Son, and the Holy Spirit are all on your side.

We often see our lives as a series of up and down moments. Some days we do good; other days we make mistakes and fail. If we rely on our own works for salvation, that is what life looks like. But if we put our faith in Jesus' perfection, allowing Him to stand in our place before God, then the Father sees our lives as one steady line at the top of the chart…because that's what Jesus' life looked like.

Once there was a man who hired a maid to clean his house. He looked through a dozen resumes and finally found a maid whose skills matched his needs. When he hired her, the two of them signed a contract that explicitly detailed their mutual obligations. He agreed to pay a certain wage in exchange for forty hours of work each week. He gave her a thick employee manual that explained her duties. The maid was required to prepare meals, wash the dishes, dust the living room, sweep the hall, and wash his clothes. The contract specified that if she failed to do her work, she would be fired.

After a time, romance blossomed between the man and the maid. They fell in love and married. After they said "I do" at the altar, the woman was no longer a servant, and the man was no longer her employer--they were now husband and wife.

As a wife, the former maid is set free from the rules and regulations of the contract. No longer does the employee manual bind her to the performance of set duties. However, because she loves her husband, she continues to do everything she used to, and even more. As a wife, her desire is to please her husband.

When there is love, no rules are required. The husband would be foolish to give her a list of Ten Marriage Commandments.

1. Thou shalt have no other husbands besides me.

2. Thou shalt not have pictures of any other men before you.

3. Thou shalt not take the name of thy husband in vain or ever say anything disrespectful about him.

4. Remember date night and keep thy schedule free so we can go out to eat.

5. Honor thy husband and thy children and take care of them.

6. Thou shalt not forget to sweep the floor, do the laundry, and cook meals.

7. Thou shalt not commit adultery.

8. Thou shalt kiss thy husband upon waking in the morning *and* before going to sleep.

9. Thou shalt not lie to thy husband.

10. Thou shalt not spend too much money at the mall.

There is a greater law in force for the wife than any Ten Commandments he could muster up. That law is love. The loving wife continues to work in the house, not out of duty, but because she cares for her husband and wants him to be happy. Nor does the husband threaten to leave her if she does not perform perfectly. When she was a maid, he could fire her for the tiniest infraction. But once they were bound together by the covenant of marriage, there was a whole new level of commitment.

Relationship, Not Rules

Another name for the law of love is the "law of the Spirit of life." Romans 8:2 refers to this law: *For the law of the Spirit of life in Christ Jesus has made me free from the law of sin and death"* (Romans 8:2).

Laws let us know when we are doing something right, and they also let us know when we are doing something wrong. In order to illustrate this, let's consider the speed limit. Often when I am driving around town, I see a sign that says, "45 MPH." This sign informs me of the speed that experts think should be maintained for that particular street.

When I was younger, I would often ignore the speed limit. I would go 55 MPH or 65 MPH. I knew I was doing wrong, but I didn't care. However, one day I was pulled over by a policeman. I received a speeding ticket. Because the ticket was so expensive, it caused me to drive more carefully. I still sped from time to time… but I kept a careful eye out for police cars.

When I became a father for the first time, I found myself much more conscious of driving safely. Now, whenever my son Caleb is in the car, I find myself driving under the speed limit. Caleb is 100% effective at making me drive the speed limit—and it's not because he is writing any tickets! In fact, with my son in the car, I don't even need any speed limit signs. I operate under a different law, the "law of protecting my son's life," the law of love.

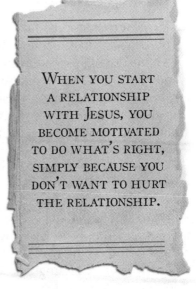

WHEN YOU START A RELATIONSHIP WITH JESUS, YOU BECOME MOTIVATED TO DO WHAT'S RIGHT, SIMPLY BECAUSE YOU DON'T WANT TO HURT THE RELATIONSHIP.

In the same way, the Law lets us know when we are doing wrong. Because disobeying the Law has consequences, it is occasionally effective at forcing us to be good. But no one can obey the Law 100% of the time. By breaking even one law, you become a lawbreaker and worthy of punishment.

But when you come out from under the Law and start a relationship with Jesus, you become motivated to do what's right, not because of the threat of punishment, but simply because you don't want to hurt the relationship. Suddenly, you are living under "the law of the Spirit of life in Christ Jesus." When my son Caleb is in the car, I drive safely, not because of the law, but because I don't want to hurt my son. Relationship is a much greater motivator than the Law could ever be.

You can do right because you obey the Law, but you can also do right apart from the Law. In this illustration, what is "right" is safe driving. The law (speed limit) can make you drive safely sometimes, but the greater law of relationship (love for your child) can motivate you to drive safely all the time.

The Law is not effective at keeping us from doing wrong. It is effective at showing us when we do wrong. Relationship is good at motivating us to do what is right. We know right and wrong because of the Law, but we know how to do right because of grace.

Law governs actions, but a grace relationship affects the heart. The Law can make you go to church, but grace compels you to worship. The Law can forbid divorce, but love between a husband and wife is a matter of relationship. The Law reduces adultery, but it can do nothing about lust. The Law can keep a person from stealing, but not from coveting. The law prevents discrimination, but not hate. In order for attitudes to change, grace is needed. My attitude toward safe driving radically changed once I had a son.

Fulfilling the Law

In the same way, there is no rule in my marriage that I have to kiss my wife. There is no law that says "Thou shalt kiss thy wife every night before going to sleep, and not just a peck, but a full blown French kiss." A kissing rule would quickly become burdensome.

No, I kiss my wife because I enjoy kissing her.

Our marriage is a relationship, not a list of rules. Legalism in marriage would take all the fun out of our relationship. In the same way, Christianity is about having a relationship with Jesus, not about keeping a list of do's and don'ts.

Life in Christ Jesus does not force us to live holy lives, rather it inspires us to live holy lives. Doing right is a delight, not a duty. I don't have to kiss my wife, I like kissing my wife. In the same way, *"His commandments are not burdensome"* (1 John 5:3).

Jesus replaced the Ten Commandments with two commandments. He said, *"'You shall love the LORD your God with all your heart, with all your soul, with all your mind, and with all your strength.' This is the first commandment. And the second, like it, is this: 'You shall love your neighbor as yourself.' There is no other commandment greater than these"* (Mark 12:30-31). Matthew 22:40 adds, *"On these two commandments hang all the Law and the Prophets"* (Matthew 22:40).

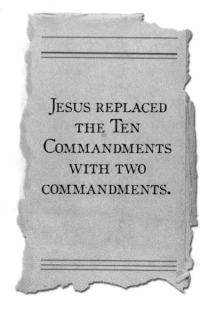

All ten commandments fall under these two commandments. Did Jesus do away with the Ten Commandments? No, He gave two better commandments that are even stronger. Why? Because now the commandments are not written on stone. God promised, *"I will engrave them on your heart"* (2 Corinthians 3:3). Instead of giving us an external list of rules that are impossible to keep, God promised, "I will put the love of God inside of you."

JESUS REPLACED THE TEN COMMANDMENTS WITH TWO COMMANDMENTS.

Under the New Covenant, you do not walk by legalism, you walk by an even higher standard than before. Is the Law passed away?

Jesus said He did not come to abolish the Law, but to fulfill it. He said, *"If you keep My commandments, you will abide in My love, just as I have kept My Father's commandments and abide in His love"* (John 15:10). We are not lawless, we are under a higher law, the law of love—the law that fulfills all the other laws.

THE MORE LOVE WE HAVE, THE LESS LAW IS NEEDED.

James calls this new law a *"perfect law of liberty"* (James 1:25). He also calls it "the royal law:" *"If you really fulfill the royal law according to the Scripture, 'You shall love your neighbor as yourself,' you do well"* (James 2:8).

The more love we have, the less Law is needed; the less there is of love, the more Law is required. Listen to what Paul says, *"Owe no one anything except to love one another, for he who loves another has fulfilled the law. For the commandments, 'You shall not commit adultery, You shall not murder, You shall not steal, You shall not bear false witness, You shall not covet,' and if there is any other commandment, are all summed up in this saying, namely, 'You shall love your neighbor as yourself.' Love does no harm to a neighbor; therefore love is the fulfillment of the law"* (Romans 13:8-10).

This does not mean we throw out the Ten Commandments. Several times, Paul mentions the Ten Commandments. For example in Ephesians 6:2, Paul tells children to honor their parents. If the Ten Commandments were passed away, why would Paul be mentioning them? However, our understanding of the Ten Commandments is to be rooted in love.

We could express the law of grace by saying, "Love God, love people." This is our new version of the Ten Commandments. However, it is impossible to do this until after you have a revelation of how much God loves you. The more you focus on how much God loves you, the more you will love Him. The more you love Him, the better you will be at loving those around you.

How will you do it? Just as God saved you by grace, He now empowers you to walk the love-walk by grace. Why do you obey God? Is it because you fear He is going to strike you dead? Or is it because you love Him and are thankful for everything He has done for you? First John 4:18 says, *"perfect love casts out fear."* We obey God's laws, but now our motive is completely different. We are not scared of punishment; we obey God's laws because of our love for Him.

St. Augustine said, "Love God and do as you please." He understood that once you love God, everything else in your life falls into its proper place. If you truly love God, you will not want to sin any longer. Love is the driving force behind grace.

Because of grace, we now have the freedom (liberty) to serve God through love. *"For you, brethren, have been called to liberty; only do not use liberty as an opportunity for the flesh, but through love serve one another"* (Galatians 5:13). Liberty from the Law is not an excuse to sin, instead it empowers us to live above the Law: *"But the fruit of the Spirit is love, joy, peace, longsuffering, kindness, goodness, faithfulness, gentleness, self-control. Against such there is no law"* (Galatians 5:22-23).

While we are indeed free from the requirements of the Old Covenant, we are only freed from a lesser law so we can serve a higher one. There is no law against love, because there is simply no higher law. Love is able to do what the Law could never do--make us blameless and holy before God. How much then should our heart's cries echo those of Paul's when he wrote, *"And may the Lord make you increase and abound in love to one another and to all, just as we do to you, so that He may establish your hearts blameless in holiness before our God and Father at the coming of our Lord Jesus Christ with all His saints"* (1 Thessalonians 3:12-13).

I like what Bono, the lead singer of the band U2, said, "And yet, along comes this idea called Grace to upend all that 'as you reap, so will you sow' stuff. Grace defies reason and logic. Love interrupts, if you like, the consequences of your actions, which in my case is very good news indeed, because I've done a lot of stupid stuff. I'm holding out for Grace. I'm holding out that Jesus took my sins onto the Cross, because I know who I am, and I hope I don't have to depend on my own religiosity."

Chapter Eighteen:
GRACE IN YOUR LIFE

In Puerto Plata, Dominican Republic, our team stayed at a beautiful hotel next to the beach. At the hotel restaurant, I struck up a conversation with the hostess.

"Are you a Christian?" I asked the young lady.

"I used to be a Christian," she replied, "but I'm not anymore."

"Why not?"

She told me her story. She said, "When I was a teenager, I attended a church that taught that women should never paint their faces with makeup or wear short skirts.

I needed a job to help feed my brothers and sisters, so I started working at a hotel. I was informed that all of the hotel staff was required to wear lipstick and knee-length skirts as part of their uniform.

When my pastor found out that I took this job, he forced me to stand in front of the congregation and tell everyone that I was no longer a Christian."

Astounded at her pastor's lack of grace, I exclaimed, "What you wear does not determine whether you are a Christian or not. Wearing makeup will not send you to hell. It is your relationship with Jesus that determines where you will spend eternity. Do you believe Jesus died on the cross for your sins? Have you made Jesus the Lord of your life?"

"Oh, I love Jesus. I talk to Him every day," she said.

"Then regardless of what your pastor told you, you are a Christian."

I prayed with her, and she left my table with a huge smile on her face.

What is Your Church Known For?

Why does the world think Christians are bigots, trying to impose their antiquated sense of morality on others? Many atheists equate fundamentalist Christians with the Islamic Taliban and accuse us of trying to drag the world back to the first century. Is this because Christians tend to be known more for what they are against than for their grace?

We are known for being anti-gay, anti-choice, anti-drinking, anti-smoking, anti-gambling, anti-R-rated movies, anti-television violence, and anti-just about everything else that the world perceives as fun. The core message of Christianity is forgiveness, love, and acceptance. But too often our message seems to be one of unforgiveness, disagreement, rejection, and hatred. Is this really what God wants the Church to be known for?

The truth is that many Christians are saved by grace, but few live by grace. Instead of focusing on grace and forgiveness, the church often preaches the Law. We put the Ten Commandments up in our schools and courthouses. We try to "impose" morality on others. Instead of offering the love of Christ, we bash people over the head with our Bibles.

Stop Enforcing Morality; Start Communicating God's Grace.

Is it feasible to attempt to impose our Christian morality on an immoral world? Can we force someone to do what is right? Can we change people's hearts by forcing them to do what is right? Should we try to impose standards on others that we cannot even uphold ourselves?

Recently in the news, I heard of a politician who resigned from office because he had an affair with one of his staff. The ironic thing is that this particular official was known for his emphasis on passing laws to promote abstinence.

No matter how "good" people are, without Jesus they are headed to hell. So, trying to force people to be "good" doesn't change their eternal destiny. Only a relationship with Jesus can change people. Jesus did not come to earth to make bad people good; He came to make dead people alive.

Trying to force someone to keep the Ten Commandments might make them look "good" on the outside, but it does not change them on the inside. The only way to effectively and eternally change people is from the inside out. So, instead of preaching on the Ten Commandments, we should preach about Jesus.

The world will never find forgiveness in two pieces of stone. We are not called to be moral people; we are called to be Jesus people. Our focus should be on Jesus, not on religious rules. Jesus never told His disciples, "Follow My rules." He told them, "Follow Me."

THE WORLD WILL NEVER FIND FORGIVENESS IN TWO PIECES OF STONE.

Don't tell people what is wrong with them; tell people what is right for them because of what Jesus accomplished on the cross. Some might protest, "But if we don't focus on teaching people to do right, then people will be worldly." Really? Then why, despite all the church's screaming and teaching about right and wrong, do people still live worldly lives?

The truth is that the only way for a person to live a godly life is through the power that comes from knowing Jesus as a personal Lord and Savior.

According to Jesus, if you have been forgiven much, you will love God much. The more you love God, the more you will want to do what is right. As soon as you realize that you have been forgiven for everything, you will want to love God with all your heart. Being aware of how much you have been forgiven will not cause you to go out and sin more, but instead it will motivate you to glorify God more with your life.

The church is most effective when it reveals God's grace. We must show grace to the world. Gordon MacDonald said, "The world can do anything the church can do except one thing: it cannot show grace."

The great evangelist D. L. Moody once said, "Of one hundred men, one will read the Bible; the ninety-nine will read the Christian." Jesus revealed how the world will recognize the believer, *"By this all will know that you are My disciples, if you have love for one another"* (John 13:35).

What are you known for? To your family? In your neighborhood? In your ministry? Are people getting a good look at Jesus when they take a look at you?

The new commandment that Jesus wants us to keep is to love one another. In this manner: *"Love one another as I have loved you"* (John 15:12). How did Christ love you? *"But God demonstrates His own love toward us, in that while we were still sinners, Christ died for us"* (Romans 5:8).

May His saints celebrate that grace till the knowledge of it fills the whole earth.

THE
FINAL
ROUND

THE FINAL ROUND

The match is almost finished. Grace needs to knock out The Law once and for all, in order to be the reigning champion of the world.

Ding, ding! The main event is on!

Today, some in the Church are cheering for Grace to win. Others are cheering for The Law to win. Some are just bewildered and don't know who to cheer for.

The fight between The Law and Grace rests in your hands. Whose side are you on? Who will win this epic battle?

After the match is over, it will be revealed that the result has been fixed. As all the saints march into heaven, it is clear that the fight between The Law and Grace has only one possible outcome.

Grace wins!

About Daniel King:

* Has spoken to more than 2,000 live audiences in over 60 nations around the world. His Gospel Festivals regularly draw crowds in excess of 50,000 people.
* Preached his first public sermon at the age of six. Grew up working with his parents as a missionary in Mexico. Started his own ministry and begin traveling to churches across America at the age of sixteen.
* Daniel recently celebrated twenty years of full-time ministry.
* Graduated summa cum laude from Oral Roberts University in 2002 with a B.A. degree in New Testament Studies and in 2014 with a Master of Divinity.
* Set a goal at the age of fifteen to lead 1,000,000 people to Jesus before the age of thirty. With God's help, Daniel has accomplished the goal of leading one million people in a prayer of salvation.
* Author of fourteen books including: *The Secret of Obed-Edom, Healing Power, Fire Power, Soul Winning,* and *Grace Wins.* Over 600,000 books in print.
* Has appeared on Daystar, TBN, TCT, Grace TV, and numerous other television and radio programs. He has been a guest lecturer at Oral Roberts University, Victory Bible College, Christ for the Nations, Lionsgate Leadership School, and The Father's House Discipleship School.
* Has built three churches overseas and trained thousands of pastors.
* Founder and President of King Ministries International.
* Co-Founder of The Soul Winner's Alliance, an organization dedicated to serving evangelists.
* Married Jessica on April 21, 2007. They have two children, Caleb and Katie Grace.

Soul Winning Festivals

Soul Winning Festivals

Metu, Ethiopia

Khushpur, Pakistan

Roca Blanca, Mexico

Sialkot, Pakistan

Agere Maryam, Ethiopia

Kisaran, Indonesia

Soul Winning Festivals

Sambava, Madagascar

Wondo Genet, Ethiopia

Kihihi, Uganda

Guder, Ethiopia

Kawdé Bouké, Haiti

Copan, Honduras

Empty Wheelchair

Set Free From Demons

Lame Walking

Tumor Gone

The Blind See

The Deaf Hear

Cripples Walk

**Miracles Prove
Jesus is Alive!**

Contact the Author:

Daniel King

daniel@kingministries.com

King Ministries International

PO Box 701113

Tulsa, OK 74170 USA

King Ministries Canada

PO Box 3401

Morinville, Alberta T8R 1S3 Canada

Visit us online at:

www.kingministries.com

Product Hotline: 1-877-431-4276

PRAYER OF SALVATION

God loves you—no matter who you are, no matter what your past. God loves you so much that He gave His one and only begotten Son for you. The Bible tells us that "...whoever believes in Him shall not perish but have eternal life" (John 3:16 NIV). Jesus laid down His life and rose again so that we could spend eternity with Him in heaven and experience His absolute best on earth. If you would like to receive Jesus into your life, say the following prayer out loud and mean it from your heart.

Heavenly Father, I come to You admitting that I am a sinner. Right now, I choose to turn away from sin, and I ask You to cleanse me of all unrighteousness. I believe that Your Son, Jesus, died on the cross to take away my sins. I also believe that He rose again from the dead so that I might be forgiven of my sins and made righteous through faith in Him. I call upon the name of Jesus Christ to be the Savior and Lord of my life. Jesus, I choose to follow You and ask that You fill me with the power of the Holy Spirit. I declare that right now I am a child of God. I am free from sin and full of the righteousness of God. I am saved in Jesus' name. Amen.

If you prayed this prayer to receive Jesus Christ as your Savior for the first time, please contact us on the Web at **www.harrisonhouse.com** to receive a free book.

Or you may write to us at

Harrison House • P.O. Box 35035 • Tulsa, Oklahoma 74153